F*ck,

I'm Bored !

Activity Book

For Adults

Featuring 100 Fucking Adult Activities: Coloring, Sudoku, Dot-to-Dot, Word Searches, Mazes, Fallen Phrases, Math Logic, Word Tiles, Spot the Difference, Where the Fuck did the Other Half Go, Nanograms, Brick-by-Fucking-Brick, Word Scramble, and Much More!

Thank you for your purchase, assholes!!
I hope you enjoy this fucking book!!

tamaraadamsauthor@gmail.com

www.tamaraladamsauthor.com

https://twitter.com/@TamaraLAdams

https://www.facebook.com/TamaraLAdamsAuthor/

http://www.amazon.com/T.L.-Adams/e/B00YSROGC4

https://www.pinterest.com/Tjandlexismom/tamara-l-adams-author/

Solve this bitch of a maze: Start in the center dot and get the fuck out!

Answer on page 101

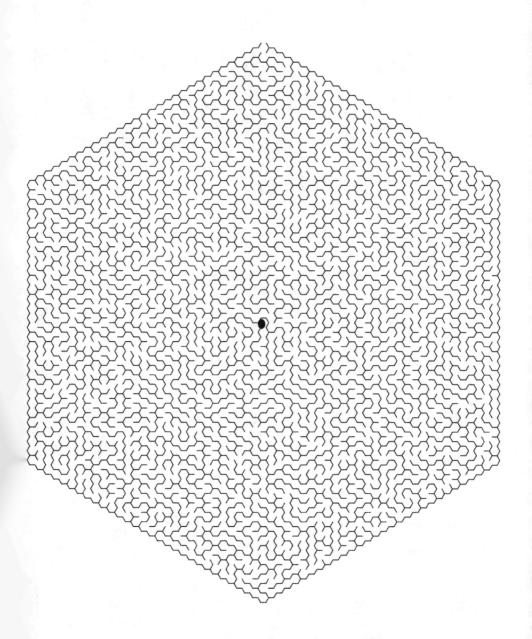

Think these pictures are the same? Think again, bitch!
Circle the 10 differences.

Answer on page 101

Search for the goddamn words in the list

Arse   Bastard   Assnugget

Boob   Caveman   Cockmaster

Egoist   Fucker   Ignoramus

Flake   Monkey   Pervert

Jerk   Grouch   Whore

Snob   Sadist   Oger

Answer on page 101

```
W Y       B X O       H P Z       D Z B       L W D
D D U       S D Q       Y G L       S Z E       G O X
  G L F       B I L       H R F       L I E       T N G
    W I L       W Y K       V O C       V X E       X B W
S       N K A       I E B       A U O       S O R       Q I
E N       Q M K       B K O       C C C       Z D O       V
B E O       C K E       A N O       Y H K       R J H
  N T B       A E E       I O B       F S M       E Z W
    U E W       V P S       O M H       G F A       G L G
I       R G S       E J R       Y T Z       S U S       O F
A T       P G C       M C A       Z R L       T C T       T
O C N       P U B       A F S       O E M       R K E
  K A E       Z N H       N D A       E V G       U E R
    R V L       U S F       C X D       D R W       N R A
G       E E I       J S X       U Q I       O E E       L E
A W       J Q C       R A Y       G Z S       I P T       R
M Q G       S H V       I P J       J H T       Z J L
  J K B       Q B O       G S Y       I K W       L G G
    I W A       P T Z       N U E       Z S H       X U S
L       C V S       Y P W       O I G       N C G       T B
C U       Z P T       U S I       R Y O       R G I       R
O Q H       X D A       F F Q       A B I       K B O
  V R G       M X R       L K R       M J S       Y R S
    T G L       N L D       O W S       U Q T       V O L
      J H A       M B E       M Q Y       S E Q       G X
```

Draw some fucking lines from 100 to 193 to see a sweet fucking picture!
Ignore the extra shit.

Answer on page 101

258 230
218 268 148 278 240
233 233 248 264 244
147 149 245 242
223 146 246
238 246 249 150 238
254 145 243 245 247 237 237
257 253 250 247 272
251 144 255 151
254 279 255 162 164 236
265 161 165
270 226 143 254
271 132 134 135 152 159 160 163 238 166 249
262 131 230 136 137 248 157 168
129 133 264 158 236 167 275
130 139 138 250 154 259 265
256 127 241 257 169 272
128 212 258 243
242 269 239
259 241 141 155 156 269 266
239 214 210
244 126 140 274 171 170 241
238 123
239 125 124 237 222 239 260
237 195 268
236 259 226 261 172 250 245
236 196 256 263
268 225 277 271
235 211 239 197 174
121 212 275 236 263
217 210 198 267 240
235 266 107 122 207 209 173 238 188 175 177
278 248
234 119 279 215 213 271 261 243 236 176 276
189 199 187 178
118 120 214 106 186 181 179
116 117 108 109 260 184 180
228 114 265 276 273 185 239 183 182
115 111 206 200
260 113 112 110 217 269 275 194 213
264 215
263 278 256 218 273 267 237 249 100
277 216 231 209 272 201 193
270 220 261 266 274 246 252
227 247 208 274 252
262 279 237 270 229 224 204 202 192
238 228 190
234 224 252 244 242 225 273 203 101 251
240 105 227 191 211
257 216 255 205 231
258 220
267 104 102 229
103 253 222
251 276 253

Ever play Sudoku? I bet your sorry ass hasn't!
These are the goddamn rules.

Answer on page 101

Numbers from 1 to 9 are inserted into sets that have 9 x 9 = 81 squares in whole. Every number can be used just once in every 3x3 block, column and row, so don't reuse that shit.

- Every number can be used just once in the blocks of 3 x 3 = 9 square blocks. Use a number more than once, you fuck everything up.
- Each row of 9 numbers ought to contain all digits 1 through 9 in any order, so don't fucking miss any.
- Every column of 9 numbers should comprise all digits 1 through 9 in any order. Hope you can fucking count.

Here's a hint for your stupid ass: One way to figure out which numbers can go in each space is to use "process of elimination" by checking to see which other numbers are already included within each square – remember, no duplicates, asshole.

8	2						9	
9		6		3	2		5	
	4			1				6
	8	3						
2		9				8		4
						5	2	
4				6			1	
	9		8	5		3		7
	7						8	2

This picture's fucked to hell! Draw each image to its corresponding square to fix that shit.

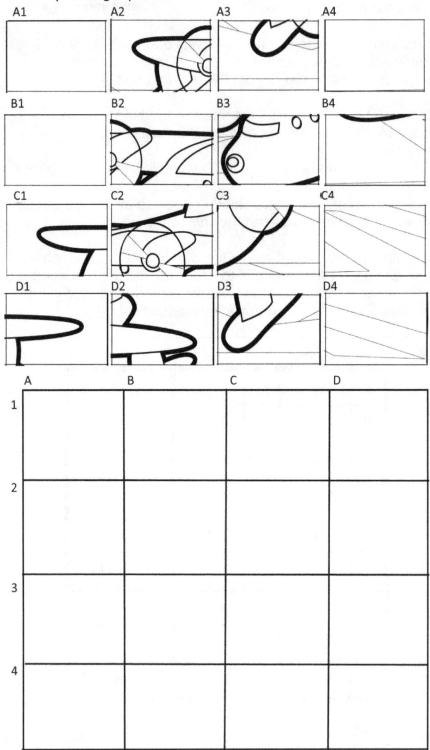

Answer on page 102

None of these words make any fucking sense. Unscramble each of the words.
Take the letters that appear in numbered boxes and unscramble them to reveal a word that describes anyone who hasn't bought this book.

Answer on page 102

KELRIRSACE

BUBBUGTELR

NIESARLSB
          4

LULOBSK
    2

HOCCROKCA

REPADSEDO

DYMPU

CCKAFUFE

NOALOHGI

SAKJSCA
    3

HEMTURFEORKC
    5

ALWOTU

PEDNKLICCI

FIFARFFR

HTDEHSAI
6

SEELGBAEZ
1

1 2 3 4 5 6

7

Draw some fucking lines from 100 to 149 to reveal a sweet fucking word! Ignore the extra shit.

Answer on page 102

258 162 201 278 240 276
218 146 147 233 248 264 245 244 243
152 157 233 246 242 238 160
238 246 223 243 245 247 249 237 272 237
254 148 253 250
257 254 255 274 149
251 279 255 239
265 143 142 236
270 226 254 275 166
271 161 230 248 185 168 167 229
262 264 258 151 209 236 249 165
238 145 144 250 259 257 169 265
256 241 272 163
242 269 239 212 243
140 241 247 141 269 266
259 239 214 210
244 139 253 208 171 138 241 267
239 262 170
159 236 222 195 239 260
237 237 226 268 164
132 259 261 172 250 133 245
236 268 225 277 196 256 263
131 211 239 130 135 271 134 156
235 197 236 174 263
212 275 240
217 210 198 188 175
235 266 153 173 238 177
207 209 236 248 176
279 278 261
279 215 213 271 189 199 187 178 179
214 186 181 180
234 128 238 129 136 273 260 137 184 183 182
228 265 276 200 126
260 127 154 217 264 206 215 269 275 194 213
263 218 273 267 237 249
277 278 256 216 231 124 193
270 220 261 116 123 266 274 246 252
115 247 125 274 252
262 117 237 270 108 107 100
150 114 118 238 122 228 225 190 224 192
234 224 252 244 242 106 202 251
119 227 191
272 113 257 216 109 255 205 101 231 211 158
267 120 121 258 105 220 268
204 110 104 273 102 229
112 227
230 251 111 276 103 203 240 222
8 155 253

Answer on page 102

How many fucking  make up the goddamn giant fist? (Don't count the one up your ass)

Solve this tit of a maze: Start in the nipple and work your way the fuck out!

Answer on page 102

Letter Tiles

Answer on page 102

I can't understand what the fuck any
of this shit says.
Move the motherfucking tiles around to
make the correct phrase.
The three letters on each tile must
stay together and in the given order,
so don't try to cheat, asshole!

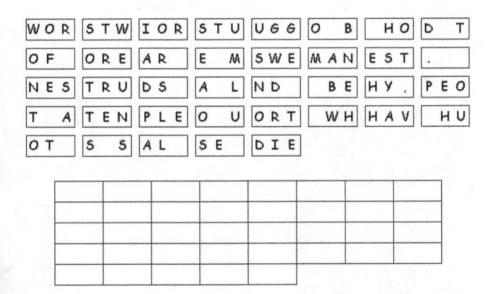

One fucking asshole always has to stand out in a crowd. Find the cunt that's different from the rest.

Answer on page 102

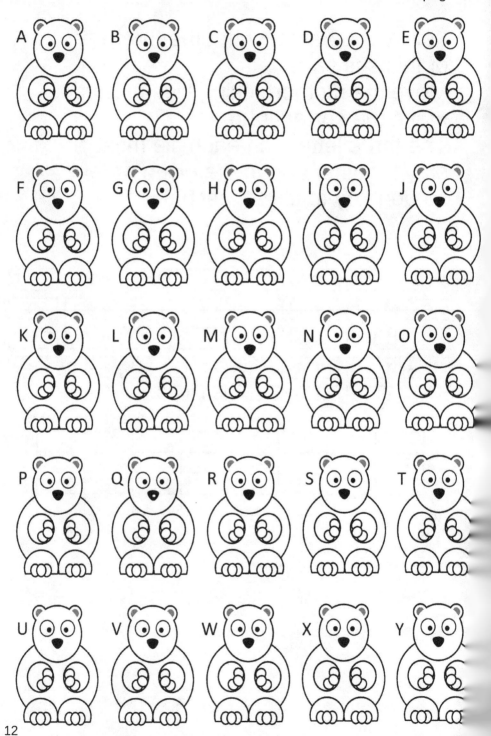

The fucked rules of a cryptogram puzzle:

You are given a shit piece of text where each letter is substituted with a irrelevant damn number and you need to fucking decide which letter in the native alphabet is being coded by the numbers you are given.

You need to use logic and knowledge of the letters and words of our goddamn language to crack this shit.

Answer on page 102

A hint for you lazy fuckers:
One of the words is *mean*

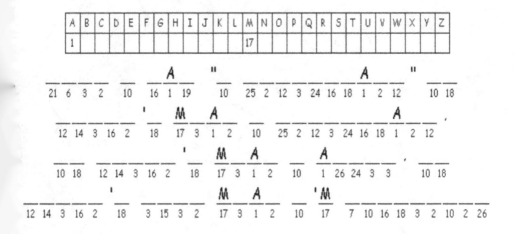

The goal of this puzzle is to figure out how the fuck you fit the numbered hexagons into the motherfucking rectangle of hexagons (that's a fuckload of geometry right there!) without changing their goddamnshape or breaking them into fucking smaller pieces.

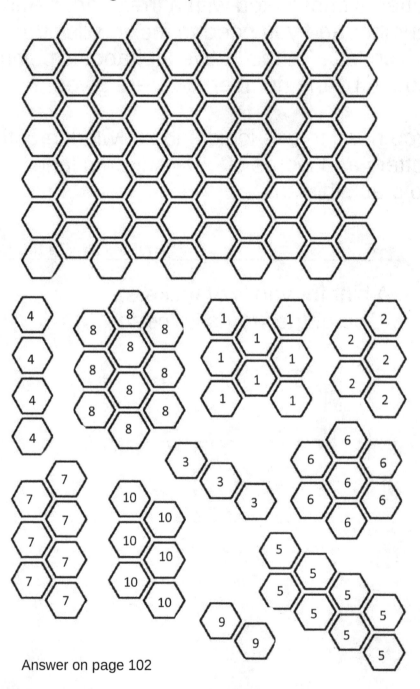

Answer on page 102

I can't read these fucking words. Unscramble the fuck out of them. Take the letters that appear in numbered boxes to reveal the word that describes your ex.

Answer on page 103

SRMTAASES   ☐☐☐☐☐☐☐☐☐☐

TICBH   ☐☐☐☐☐

RABTINRAF   ☐☐☐[4]☐☐☐☐☐

CANNIBLA   ☐☐☐☐☐☐☐☐

CKCEHNI   ☐☐☐☐☐☐☐

DORDAHLET   ☐☐☐☐☐☐☐[1]☐

ODBUM   ☐☐☐☐☐

COGFUNNIKG   ☐☐☐☐[2]☐☐☐☐☐

PUYML   ☐☐☐☐☐

DAETNLAERHN   ☐☐☐[3]☐☐☐☐☐☐☐☐

COILIDK   ☐☐☐☐☐☐☐

PIPRER   ☐☐☐☐☐☐

TESRIAHET   ☐☐☐☐☐☐☐☐☐

SEIDNRLW   ☐☐[5]☐☐☐☐☐☐

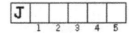

J					
	1	2	3	4	5

15

Color your ass off!

Ever play Sudoku? I bet your ridiculous ass hasn't!
Here are the mother fucking rules.   Answer on page 103

Numbers from 1 to 9 are inserted into sets that have 9 x 9 = 81 squares in whole. Every number can be used just once in every 3x3 block, column and row, so don't reuse that shit.

- Every number can be used just once in the blocks of 3 x 3 = 9 square blocks. Use a number more than once, you fuck shit up.
- Each row of 9 numbers ought to contain all digits 1 through 9 in any order, so don't leave out any numbers, asshole.
- Every column of 9 numbers should comprise all digits 1 through 9 in any order. Hope you got all that that shit.

Here's a hint jackass: One way to figure out which numbers can go in each space is to use "process of elimination" by checking to see which other numbers are already included within each square – remember, no duplicates, dumbass.

	8	7	6				3	
5			1		8	7		2
		3		2				
	1					6		
	9	5				3	1	
		6					4	
				7		1		
6		8	5		3			7
	3				4	5	8	

The damn goal consists of finding the black boxes in each grid.

The numbers given on the side and top of the grid indicate the numbers of consecutive black boxes in each line or column. Got that, bitches?

Here's a goddamn example: 3,3 on the left of a line indicates that there is, from left to right, a block of 3 black boxes then a block of 3 black boxes on this line. Have I lost your ass yet?
To solve the puzzle, you need to determine which cells will be black and which will be fucking empty. Determining which cells are to be left empty (called spaces) is as important as determining which to fill (called boxes). Later in the solving process, the spaces help determine where a clue (continuing block of boxes and a number in the legend) may spread. Solvers usually use a dot or a cross to mark cells they are certain are spaces.

It is also important never to fucking guess. Only cells that can be determined by damn logic should be filled. An example is shown here:

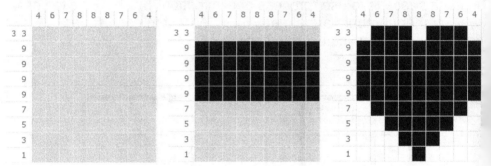

Answer on page 103

Number Blocks

Answer on page 103

Try to fill in the missing numbers if you can, bitch!

The missing numbers are integers (that means it's a whole number, dumbass) between 0 and 9.
The numbers in each row add up to the totals to the right. The numbers in each column add up to the totals along the bottom. Numbers can be repeated, so don't get fucking confused! Keep it simple, stupid.
The diagonal lines also add up the totals to the right.
Good fucking luck!

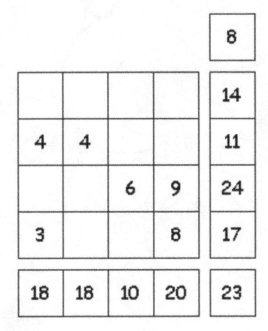

Holy shit, that's a lot of circles! Someone should keep track of this shit. Count up all the circles in the egg.

Answer on page 103

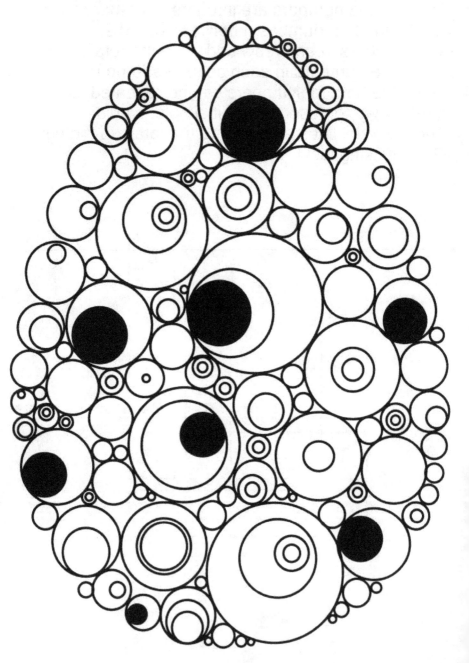

Draw some motherfucking lines from 100 to 156 to reveal a magnificent fucking picture! Ignore the extra shit.

Answer on page 103

287
248   259   247 293 238   297   296   265
273   270 192 265 279 263   295
267   261 266   254   264
268   111 112   253 214   168   235
266   217
249 246 273   113 261 215   114 115   251 191
210 110   172 268   243   257
174 271   275 258   204   181
109 169   274   223   190   282 250 263
275 171   228 272   195 189 182
205   230   175   229   196 188   283   116
108   176 270 194   227   187 183
243   232 202   184   252
245 151 233   247   117
249 152   303 201 197 186 185   180
222 107   153 254 251 300   184   276
106   290 200 198   170 122
239   150   241 199   285 93 177   118
248
179   240 239   246 277 178 221 123
212 149   237 134   218
240 154   279 302 164 220 219 280
105   209   239 143 242 135   119
225 155 100 101 160   244   133   129 252 121
238 104 156   291 159   136 231 244 226 124
102   142   132   253 157 120
224 103   148 144   236 137 238   161 128
236   141 131 262 130   125
259 241   147
286 166 260 146   145 140 167 138   213 127 237 236
165   237   126
278 208   242 207 256 269 139   274   211 163 158 255 267
173   239   277 162
216 206 236   276 238 272 257 260 269 234
264 301   250 294 289   288   281
258 262 271 292 237   299 298 284   256

21

Fallen Phrases

Answer on page 103

A fallen phrase is a fucked puzzle where all the letters have fallen to the bottom. They got jacked up on their way down, but remain in the same row. Complete this horse shit by filling the letters in the column they fall under. You start by filling in the one-letter columns, because those clearly don't have anywhere else to go in their column, dumbass. Don't make this shit harder than it has to be.
Also try filling in common one-, two- and three-letter words. I even gave your lucky ass an example.

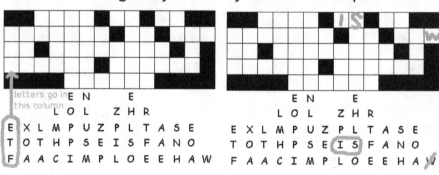

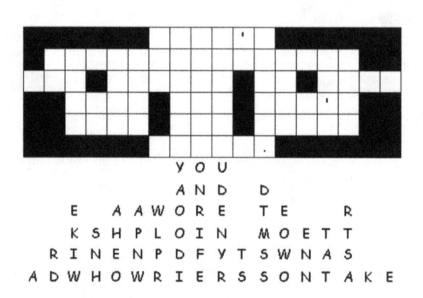

Where'd the other motherfucking half go?
Draw that shit.

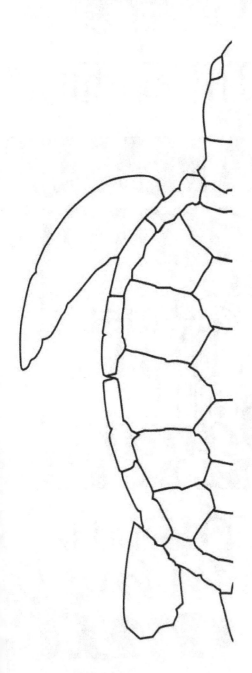

How many Dammits can you find, god dammit?

Answer on page 103

Dammit
Dammit
Dammit
Dammit
Dammit
Dammit
Dammit
Dammit
DAMMIT
Dammit
Dammit
Dammit
Dammit
DAMMIT
Dammit
Dammit
Dammit
Dammit
DAMMIT
Dammit
Dammit
Dammit
Dammit
Dammit

Solve the wanker of a maze. Start at the opening on the right side and work your way to the center of that shit.

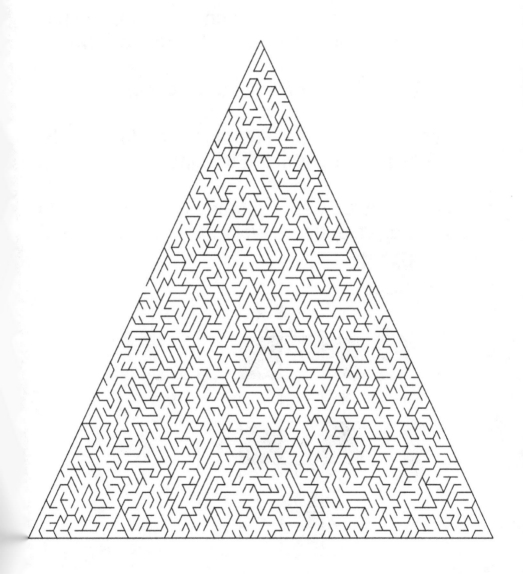

Answer on page 104

Math Squares

Answer on page 104

Try to fill in the missing numbers, bitch!

Use the numbers 1 through 9 to complete the equations. Not good at math? You're fucked.

Each number is only used once, got it?

Each row is a math equation. Good luck with that shit. Work from left to right.

That's not all! Each column is a math equation, too. Surprise, bitch! Work from top to bottom.

	+		×		10
+	■	/	■	×	
	+		-		6
+	■	+	■	-	
	×		+		33
17		7		4	

Color that shit up!

Search for all these shitty words in the Triangle below.

Answer on page 103

Crap
Dung
Feces
Stool
Shart
Shit

Poop
Manure
Excretion
Waste
Deuce

Defecation
Discharge
Excrement
Feculence
NumberTwo

```
                              J  N
                              V  N
                           G  A  F  X
                           W  X  F  D
                        A  S  P  E  Z  K
                        u  H  O  C  C  K
                     H  S  A  O  E  N  K  A
                     L  J  R  P  S  M  N  O
                  Y  P  Y  T  S  O  S  N  C  D
                  Y  G  B  E  T  L  O  M  G  O
               M  E  X  X  X  L  A  O  E  L  V  C
               L  E  Z  K  N  L  E  R  O  H  R  V
            Q  J  T  R  U  U  B  X  A  T  T  C  E  H
            F  E  S  K  K  M  S  C  M  B  D  S  M  I
         D  C  V  A  C  Y  B  O  R  N  J  E  F  Z  C  T
         X  M  K  W  G  M  E  G  E  Z  S  S  L  L  X  D
      u  L  Y  F  C  P  G  R  J  T  B  X  H  O  Q  Q  A  F
      I  R  T  C  O  L  V  T  B  I  R  P  Q  L  V  F  X  H
   K  F  u  W  I  W  C  A  W  G  O  E  C  u  E  D  M  P  E  F
   N  Q  Y  X  T  H  Y  E  O  R  N  S  O  N  J  G  A  M  Z  B
H  P  F  K  E  G  S  S  L  Q  W  X  X  F  O  S  R  R  R  P  R  L
H  L  Q  X  Y  D  Z  I  R  G  D  M  E  J  I  C  Z  S  A  P  V  C
K  Z  S  C  H  J  K  P  I  u  I  M  J  X  G  T  J  I  Y  B  H  B  L  T
H  S  R  G  N  u  D  E  Q  O  Y  I  R  F  S  A  R  A  Y  F  G  C  M  V
K  X  E  C  Y  J  S  X  L  K  T  T  L  N  F  B  C  J  M  E  G  Z  E  S  P  X
X  M  E  P  R  J  I  L  V  X  Y  K  F  Q  Z  X  E  H  Z  R  C  u  J  M  I  O
J  E  G  Q  K  A  B  V  Y  S  R  E  R  u  N  A  M  F  I  O  S  E  A  Q  R  E  D  G
N  M  Q  F  V  u  S  K  u  O  M  D  F  E  C  u  L  E  N  C  E  L  F  Z  N  A  Q  O
T  A  Y  T  H  S  W  J  P  G  E  J  u  X  R  X  L  E  D  D  E  O  K  V  K  E  Z  N  Y  I
J  F  G  V  B  S  Q  K  C  N  I  S  T  G  X  X  P  Q  A  F  Z  R  Y  E  R  M  G  V  A
```

Letter Tiles

Answer on page 103

I can't understand this shit!

Move the fucking tiles around to
make the correct phrase.

The three letters on each tile must
stay together and in the given order,
so don't try to cheat, motherfucker!

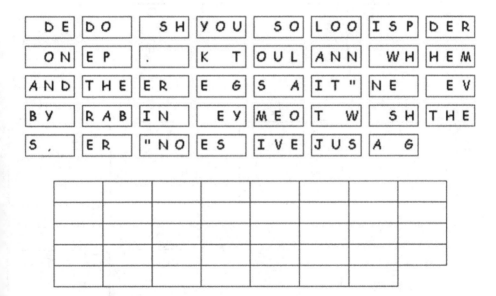

D E	D O		S H	Y O U	S O	L O O	I S P	D E R
O N	E P	.	K T	O U L	A N N	W H	H E M
A N D	T H E	E R	E G	S A	I T "	N E	E V
B Y	R A B	I N	E Y	M E O	T W	S H	T H E
S ,	E R	" N O	E S	I V E	J U S	A G	

One fucking cunt always has to be the difficult one. Find the asshole that's different from the rest.

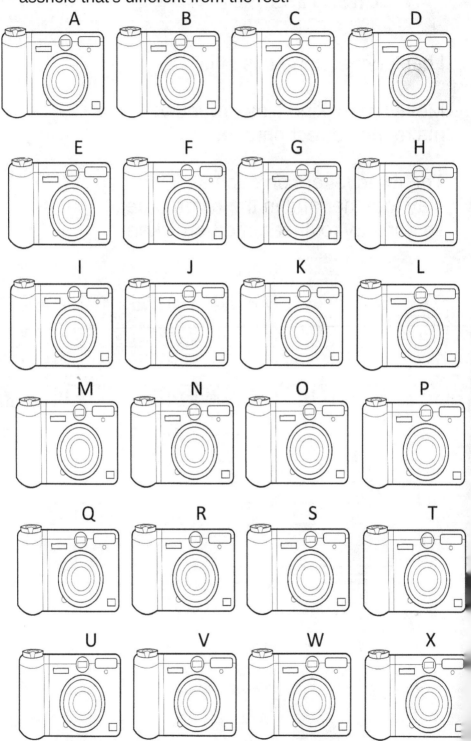

Answer on page 104

Fallen Phrases

Answer on page 103

A fallen phrase is a fucked puzzle where all the letters have fallen to the bottom. They got jacked up on their way down, but remain in the same row. Complete this horse shit by filling the letters in the column they fall under. You start by filling in the one-letter columns, because those clearly don't have anywhere else to go in their column, dumbass. Don't make this shit harder than it has to be.

Also try filling in common one-, two- and three-letter words. I even gave your lucky ass an example.

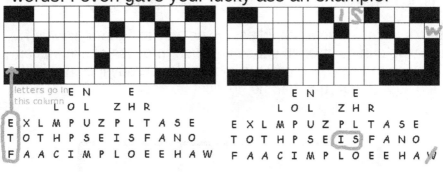

```
letters go in    E  N        E
this column    L  O  L     Z  H  R
 E  X  L  M  P  U  Z  P  L  T  A  S  E
 T  O  T  H  P  S  E  I  S  F  A  N  O
 F  A  A  C  I  M  P  L  O  E  E  H  A  W
```

```
              E  N        E
            L  O  L     Z  H  R
 E  X  L  M  P  U  Z  P  L  T  A  S  E
 T  O  T  H  P  S  E  I  S  F  A  N  O
 F  A  A  C  I  M  P  L  O  E  E  H  A
```

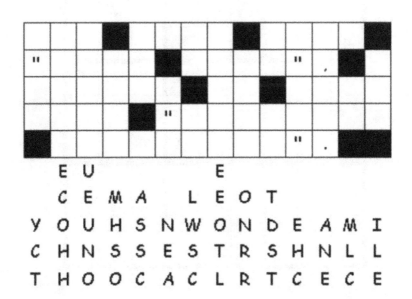

```
   E  U                 E
   C  E  M  A     L  E  O  T
Y  O  U  H  S  N  W  O  N  D  E  A  M  I
C  H  N  S  S  E  S  T  R  S  H  N  L  L
T  H  O  O  C  A  C  L  R  T  C  E  C  E
```

Ever play Sudoku? I bet your sorry ass hasn't!
These are the goddamn rules. Answer on page 104

Numbers from 1 to 9 are inserted into sets that have 9 x 9 = 81 squares in whole. Every number can be used just once in every, 3x3 block, column and row, so don't reuse that shit.

- Every number can be used just once in the blocks of 3 x 3 = 9 square blocks. Use a number more than once, you fuck everything up.
- Each row of 9 numbers ought to contain all digits 1 through 9 in any order, so don't fucking miss any.
- Every column of 9 numbers should comprise all digits 1 through 9 in any order. Hope you can fucking count.

Here's a hint for your stupid ass: One way to figure out which numbers can go in each space is to use "process of elimination" by checking to see which other numbers are already included within each square – remember, no duplicates, asshole.

		8						
	7	1					2	
4			6		9		5	
2	3	7	8		4			5
	8						7	
1			2		3	9	8	4
	4		9		2			7
	5					3	4	
						6		

Solve the maze, bitch. Start in the slit at the top and get the fuck down to the bottom.

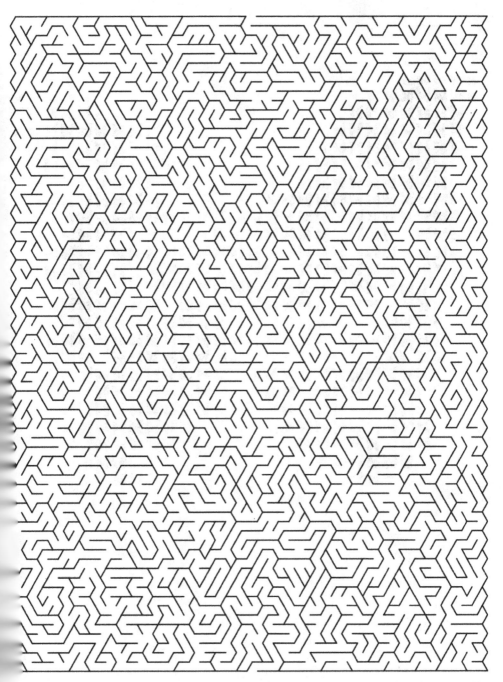

How many fucking cheery-ass butterflies can you find?

Answer on page 104

I can't read any of these damn words. Unscramble this shit.
Then use the letters that appear in the numbered boxes to
reveal words that describes this fucking book.

Answer on page 105

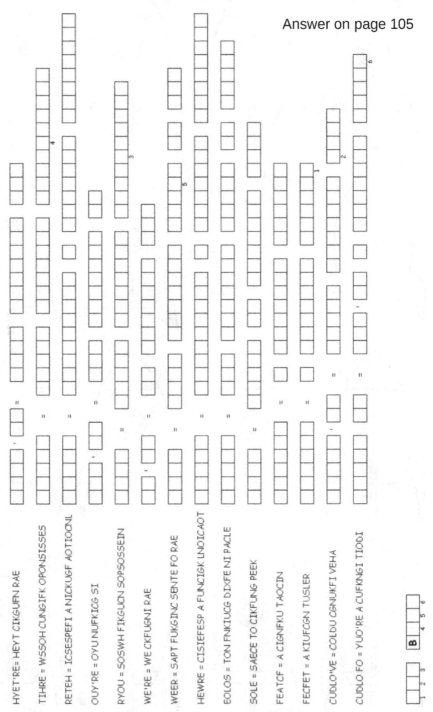

HYET'RE = HEY T CIKGUFN RAE

TIHRE = WSSOH CUNGIFK OPONSISSES

RETEH = ICSESPEFI A NICKU6F AOTIOCNL

OUY'RE = OYU NUFKICG SI

RYOU = SOSWH FIKGUCN SOPSOSSEIN

WE'RE = WE CKFUGNI RAE

WEER = SAPT FUKGINC SBNTE FO RAE

HEWRE = CISIEFESP A FUNCIGK LNOICAOT

EOLOS = TON FNKIUCG DIXFE NI PACLE

SOLE = SAECE TO CIKFUNG PEEK

FEATCF = A CIGNFKU TAOCIN

FECFET = A KIUFCGN TUSLER

CUDLO'VE = COLDU CGNUKFI VEHA

CUDLO FO = YUO'RE A CUFKNGI TIODI

35

One fucking asshole always has to be different. Find that cunt.

Answer on page 105

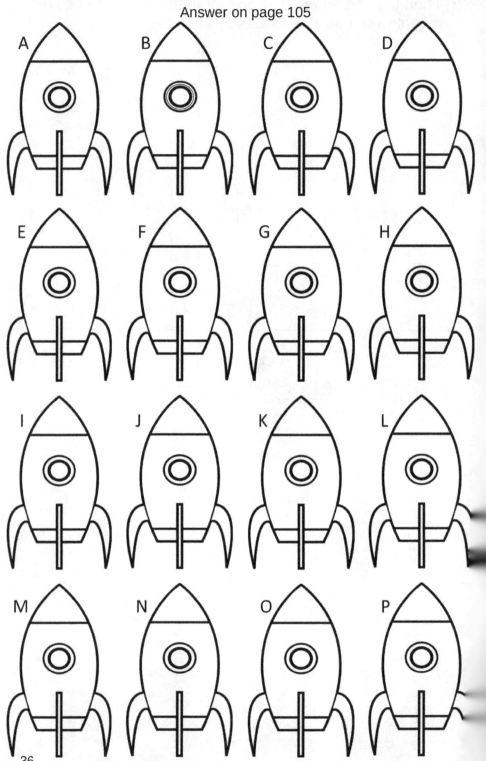

Search for the fucked up words, wanker.

Bandit   Boozer   Asskisser
Dummy   Cheater   Hillbilly
Eunuch   Sleaze   Monster
Fibber   Oldfart   Reject
Conman   Varmint   Weirdo

```
M Q X J P    S X T          A Y C    D U B K R
U H D O A    M X D          S L G    T Q T S E
M I H M Y    I D J          S L L    Z Q T A Z
V F C        D V G          K I F      U C O
U D U        R W E          I B K      Z L O
D T N        Z L B          S L C    J B B
A U U        Y W P          S L A    B T D
H I E        J Y A          E I E    U P I
P U L        V B M          R H P    O L C
A M M        I V E F B G E K Q E    Q N H
V C Q        R Q K V A R M I N T    S K V
S R B        W L M S R Z J W O Q    B G C
L D C        C R D          V L T    G J H
E P M        M E W          F D W    P M E
A U C        O J E          Y F N    H K A
Z N C        N E I          M A D    B B T
E K O        S C R          Z R U    V A E
C L R        T T D          Y T M    C N R
C C E        E D O          C F M    K D Y
O Q B        R F U          Q I Y      I I F
N I B        Q I Y          T H S      H T T
M T I X A                            D X B V Y
A R F V A                            O L G X B
N W J A A                            P L Y H C
```

The other half is gone, bitch.
You need to draw it back in or we are
all fucked!

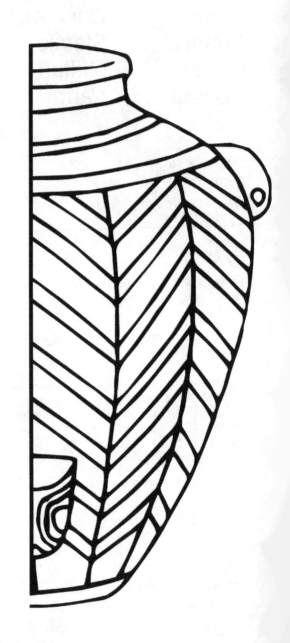

Connect the damn numbers from 100 to 139
The other fucking numbers are extra, so don't get fucked by them!

Answer on page 105

255　121　266
248　174
250　　237　120　122　241
242　241　245　239
114　115　239　119　256　247　267
270　238　243　240　116　258　259　123
258　257　265　239　118　257　155　246
112　117　242　124　249
271　113　111　238　164　173　245
262　125　160　156
279　276　244　194
272　271　157
237　278　235　274　126　127　270　158
263　268　273　128
223　193
140　261　234　276　177
110　233　133　129
260　238　165　163
225　172　279
222　161　272　132　166　244
269　228　230　171
255　267　224　226　175　134　131　263　261
109　159　217　229　170　169　168　167　162　130
264　218　216　176　274
153　181　260　269
220　227　215　273　180　183　182　154
145　135
249　246　214　212　184　236　247　195
108　248　210　179
107　243　275　237
240　209　211　136　213　178　185　238
104　236
106　137　236　277　192
105　239　237　103　186　264　191
278　277　207　206　205
265　254　275　138　190　196
102　266　187
188　208　204　149　197
262　253　252　189　198
101　139　250　148　144　150
236　201　254　100　147　203　199　256
253　251　146　143　151
268　252　141　259
142　200
251　152　202

39

Think these pictures are the same? Think again, asshole!
Circle the 13 differences, then check to see if you're right.

Answer on page 105

40

Answer on page 106

Start in the middle and find your way
the fuck out of this shit!

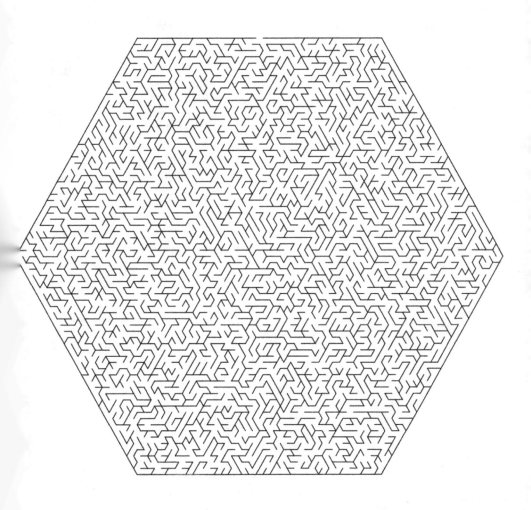

Connect the fucking numbers from 100 to 130

Answer on page 106

Don't let the extra damn numbers fool your dumb ass!

230
218 101 102   278 240   276   162
159   258   233 268 233 248 264   245   244   243
  138   242
238   246   223 137 246   238
257   254   243 245 247 249   237   237
251 100 104 103 136   253   250   272 153
  265   254   279 255 255 274   236 239
271   230 226   254 151 275 166   141
262 270 105 106 248   185   168 167 249
   238 111 264 107 258   135 236   156
256   241   250   259   257 169 272 265
   242 269 239   212   243   139
259 239   241 108 214   247   269 266
244   110 109   262 171   210   267
   239 253   222   195 239   170 241
158   237 226 261   268   260
237 236 259 113 112   172 250 245 270
236 268 225   116 256   263
235   211 239 277 196 271 174
   157 212 210   197 275 236   263
217   209 198 173 238 188 175 240
235   266 207 114 115 278   236 248 176 177
   279   215   271   261   187 178
209   214 213   189 199   186 181 179
150 234 238   276 124 273 260   180
   228   265 123 125 200 184 183 182
260   161 217 264 206 117 269   213
263   122   215   275 194
   278 256   218 273 267 237 249 154
277 220 261 216 121 231 118 201   193
270   227 247 120 266 274 246 252
262 279   119 208   224   274 252
   142   238 237 228   225 190 202 192 251
152 234 224 252 244 242   191
272 140 257 155 216 126 227 127   211 146
   134   255 205 231
163 267   204   258 133 132 129 128   220 148
144 251   160 229   229 222
   147 145 143 276   253   273 203 149
165   164 131 130 240
42

This picture's fucking fucked! Draw each image to it's correct square to fix the the motherfucker.

Answer on page 106

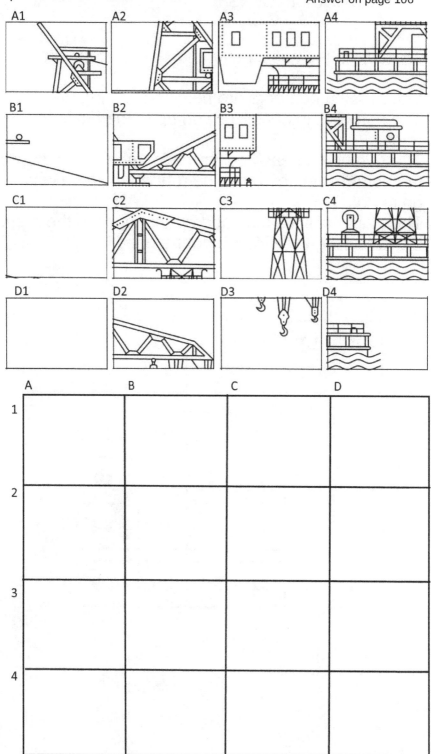

Answer on page 106

Try to fill in the missing numbers if you can, bitch!

The missing numbers are between fucking 0 and 12.
The numbers in each row add up to the totals to the right.
The numbers in each column add up to the totals along the bottom. Numbers can be repeated, so do what you gotta do!
The diagonal lines also add up the totals to the right.
Good fucking luck! You're gonna need it.

					47
14	12	9		10	53
			10		34
1		8		10	33
		1	3	1	19
9	13	1		0	24
31	41	31	34	26	29

Think these pictures are the same? You're wrong, bitch!
Circle the 10 differences.

Answer on page 106

45

Have fun coloring, assholes!

Answer on page 106

This shit is fucked!

Move the jacked tiles around to
make the correct fucking phrase.

The three letters on each tile must
stay the fuck together and in the given order,
so don't try to cheat, you wanker!

E N D	B E	R L	N E S	A N	C O	T H	B E
Y Y	C U	H E E	N C Y	N D E	I C	D S	R C A
R T O	A C K	C O	O U R	, R	A N	S T I	O F
M M O	F R I	W E	U L D	U D E	L B	T E L	M M E
E C E	S H O	A T	N T S	S T	S .	S A	N D

Search for the words, jackass

Baby
Bum
Fuck
Nuts
Swine

Clown
Cretin
Devil
Lucky
Slave

Asshole
Grumpy
Mutant
Pavian
Weezebag

```
            F Q V
          N W R O U U I C C
        O K W B N X W G C T X X D
    W Q G Y G B C D A M X W D A M A E
    T W M P J L I V E D S A Y A J Y Y O W
  C M U F D N E U W K T Y D S O C Q S V C L
  L M P V M A C J S M X B I A S X Y W V T H
N O B A W H W Y I T U J Q P C F H I O M Y Y X
U W R E U N J J C A W H K K O W A O E Q Y P I
B P N X M H S Y P O X D P Q Z A B V E L E M F Z V
F X K E N S Y O P W T J A M W Z C G E Y E T X T S
S G D F V R T S A M K U A F Z Q A R Z M F V G C J
U B L L Y Z A W V V H H C C W V K W U Z E H B L M O O
R O E A U B H L O I N P K U J N R K M D A N Y O W C J
M F M K Y H U A S A I B S L F D E G P I Y T I H M E C
R O U U K S F Q N T U S G U Y X H Y Y Y A L W Z B
S N R B F K O W E E Z E B A G T B Y G B Y A U S M
A D D N M A P S N R Y U H I Y J F R H R Z Z J I Z
N W L Q Y U M J C A S H Z W E N V C J B H U M
V E Q X X K S E H M Z Z A S B Y A M U T A N T
  Q N T D P C F P P F A M H E B A B Y A R C
  T Z Y V Z T U V Q M T C Z T B K N M O V T
    K X M D S Y L M I J U A T Q L E O M S
      U F G P T Z Y L L F B E J T H V F
        R J N U J T T S G V N J B
          C E N Y L K W W A
            Y P T
```

Answer on page 107

Find the motherfucker that's different from the rest.

Answer on page 107

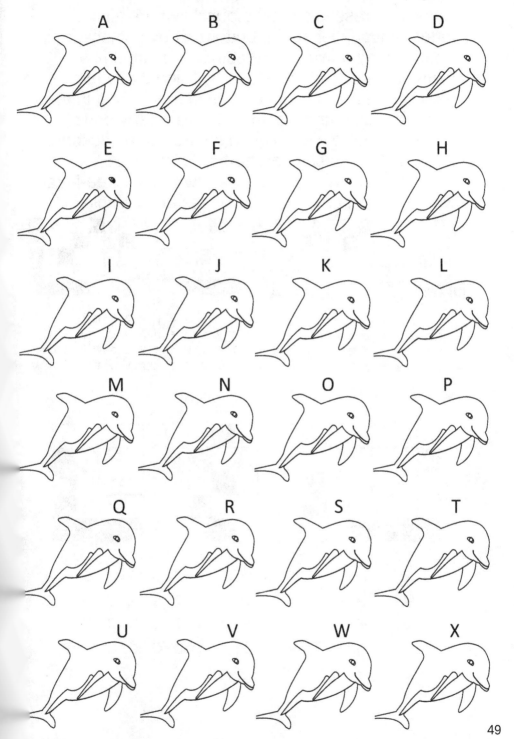

49

Fallen Phrases

Answer on page 107

A fallen phrase is a fucked puzzle where all the letters have fallen to the bottom. They got jacked up on their way down, but remain in the same row. Complete this fucked puzzle by filling the letters in the column they fall under. You start by filling in the one-letter columns, because those clearly don't have anywhere else to go in their column, jackbass. Don't make this shit harder than it has to be.

Also try filling in common one-, two- and three-letter words. I even gave your lucky ass an example.

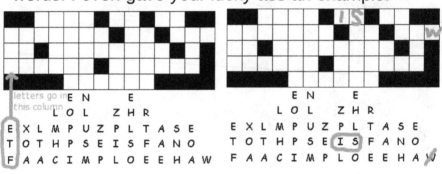

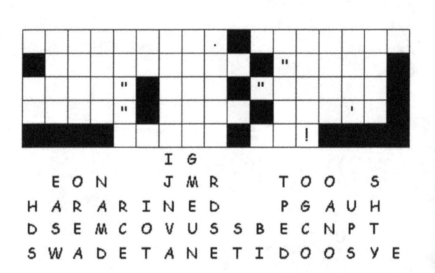

Math Squares

Answer on page 107

Try to fill in the missing numbers, wanker!

Use the numbers 1 through 16 to complete the equations. Not good at math…get your ass back to school.

Each number is only used once, so don't fuck it up!

Each row is a math equation, good luck with that shit. Work from left to right.

That's not all! Each column is also a math equation, too. Surprise, bitch. This is too much fucking math, but if your gonna do it, work from top to bottom.

	-		-		-		**-14**
-	■	+	■	×	■	×	
	+		+		×		**73**
×	■	-	■	-	■	/	
	-		×		/		**-25**
+	■	+	■	-	■	-	
	-		-		-		**-16**
-103		**19**		**-6**		**10**	

Answer on page 107

Solve the maze, asswipe. Start in the opening at the top and work your way to the opening at the goddamn bottom.

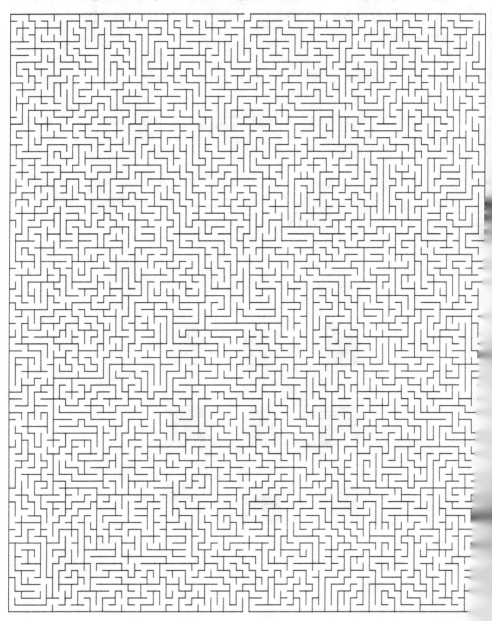

Ever play Sudoku? I bet you fucking haven't! These are the wanked rules.

Answer on page 107

Numbers from 1 to 9 are inserted into sets that have 9 x 9 = 81 squares in whole. Every number can be used just once in every, 3x3 block, column and row, so don't reuse the goddamn shit.

- Every number can be used just once in the blocks of 3 x 3 = 9 square blocks. Use a number more than once, your fucked.
- Each row of 9 numbers must fucking contain all digits 1 through 9 in any order, so don't fucking miss that shit.
- Every column of 9 numbers should comprise all digits 1 through 9 in any order. Hope you can fucking count, bitch.

Here's a hint for your stupid ass: One way to figure out which numbers can go in each space is to use "process of elimination" by checking to see which other numbers are already included within each square – remember, no duplicates, asshole.

				7	4	2		6
	2	4	6		3		7	
				2		5		9
						8		
	5		2		6		1	
		3						
2		5		1				
	1		4		5	9	6	
8		9	7	6				

Letter Tiles

Answer on page 107

What the fuck is this shit?!

Move the piece of shit tiles around to make the correct phrase.

The three letters on each tile must stay together and in the given order, so don't try to cheat, motherfucker!

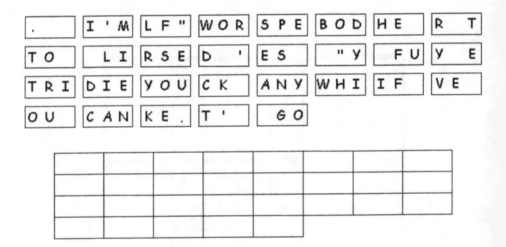

.		I ' M	L F "	W O R	S P E	B O D	H E	R T
T O		L I	R S E	D '	E S	" Y	F U	Y E
T R I	D I E	Y O U	C K	A N Y	W H I	I F	V E	
O U	C A N	K E ,	T '	G O				

Think these pictures are the same? Wrong answer, asshole! Circle the 10 differences.

Answer on page 108

Draw some damn lines from 100 to 155
Don't let the extra numbers fuck you up!

Answer on page 108

254   255
          169   273   271   211   270
274   275
236   253   252   213   210   114   207
230   272   250   247   113   115
          251   156   266   241   239   215
          244   242   253   215
212   249   246   112   209   248   116
235   234   254   265   255
247   243   237   248   277   251
          245   243   213   210
239   168
224   231   236   252   249   211
244   242   241   262   251   250   238
238   240   239   264   157   158   162
          235   237   111   260
226   110   249   246   163   117
214   238   236   239   246   268   217   248   225   164   264
228   109   236   245   243   262   259   266
220   257   231   265   166
191   108   227   258
227   237   241   165   236   268   118
223   228   240   277   240   239   237   167
229   264   234   274   226   275   272   256   171
          107   239   229   274   174   173   172
222   149   208   236   271   275
217   273   272   237   175   119
245   218   142   271   270   238   120   176   273
          262   159   134   133   126   177   19
242   214   150   279   276   124   193
224   106   225   160   125   206   194   178   25
190   135   278   279
238   279   277   212   263   127   276   121   179
105   151   143   161   278   203
263   278   148   141   136   261   263   122   27
276   265   260   269   132   267   123   180
102 103 104 152 216   199   131   128   204   181
153   147   193   140   129   261
101   260   269   267   233   268   137   259   130   129   269   267   195   250   24
154   144   266   194   139   138   258   202   196   182
155   259   146   145   201   197   220   183   255
100   252   195   223   200   198   184   1
          257 258   209   257   185   254
222   261   205   189   186   233
218   256   247   256   188   187
192   230   190

56

Look! Another tit maze! Start in the center and work your way out at the top. Don't get fucking lost or your fucked.

Answer on page 108

How many fucking fucked up hearts can you find in the image?

Answer on page 108

Draw the other fucking half.

Answer on page 108

I can't read these piece of shit words. Unscramble the motherfuckers. Then use the damn letters that appear in numbered boxes to reveal a word that describes your boss.

Answer on page 108

SOELSHA ☐☐☐☐☐☐☐

MEOGABNY ☐☐☐☐☐☐☐

TASROUNROSUB ☐☐☐☐☐☐☐☐☐☐
_2_

TUNHACVISI ☐☐☐☐☐☐☐☐☐☐
_1_

MAMDIT ☐☐☐☐☐☐

CAHEKIDD ☐☐☐☐☐☐☐
_3_

LRNAICIM ☐☐☐☐☐☐☐

KURNDRAD ☐☐☐☐☐☐☐

BIISITTHEINOX ☐☐☐☐☐☐☐☐☐☐☐☐☐

TGNERGAS ☐☐☐☐☐☐☐☐

CESRHRUFKOE ☐☐☐☐☐☐☐☐☐☐

MLNISNIKSIG ☐☐☐☐☐☐☐☐☐☐

TAENINSISPHA ☐☐☐☐☐☐☐☐☐☐☐☐

DORWY ☐☐☐☐☐
_5_

BUSKAZG ☐☐☐☐☐☐
_4_

TASBDMIARYLS ☐☐☐☐☐☐☐☐☐☐☐

RWWLFELLAO ☐☐☐☐☐☐☐☐☐☐

☐☐☐☐☐
1 2 3 4 5

This pictures fucking jacked! Draw each image to it's corresponding square to fix that goddman shit. Answer on page 108

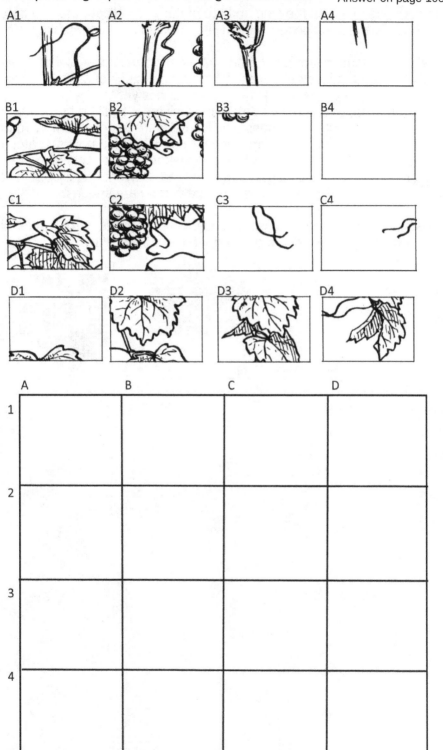

The damn goal consists of finding the black boxes in each grid.

The numbers given on the side and top of the grid indicate the numbers of consecutive black boxes in each line or column. Got that, bitches?

Here's a goddamn example: 3,3 on the left of a line indicates that there is, from left to right, a block of 3 black boxes then a block of 3 black boxes on this line. Have I lost your ass yet?

To solve a puzzle, one needs to determine which cells will be black and which will be fucking empty. Determining which cells are to be left empty (called spaces) is as important as determining which to fill (called boxes). Later in the solving process, the spaces help determine where a clue (continuing block of boxes and a number in the legend) may spread. Solvers usually use a dot or a cross to mark cells they are certain are spaces.

It is also important never to fucking guess. Only cells that can be determined by damn logic should be filled. An example is shown here:

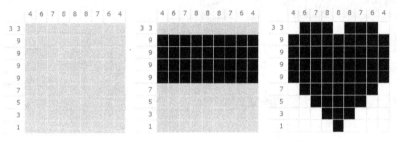

Answer on page 108

		8	1 1	1	0	8	1	8	0	8	1 1	1 1	0	8	2	2 2	1 1
3 1 1 3 1 1																	
1 1 1 1 1 1																	
2 1 1 1 1 1																	
1 1 1 1 2																	
1 1 1 1 2																	
1 1 1 1 1 1																	
1 1 1 1 1 1																	
1 3 3 1 1																	

Hey wanker! Draw lines from 100 to 180
Don't let the extra numbers fuck with your head!

Answer on
page 109

230
218   258   278   240   276   237
268   248 264 245   244   243
233
101   102 107   246   108   120   242   137   138
223   119   249   121
238   246   243 245   247   125 124 237 136 238   139
254   253   274   272 143 142
251 257   254   255   255   126 123 122 135 144 239
265   279   254   275   141 140
270   226
271   248 118 185
230   187 236 249 250
262   238   264
256 104 103   258   127 130 131 265 145
241   250 113 114   257   134
242 269 239 212 259 117 243 272
259   241   214   247   266 233
244 239   112   115 116   210 269 132 133 267
253   222 262   129   146
239   239 128 149
100 105   106 109 111 195 110 148 260 147
237   237   268 245
236 236 259 226 261 250
236 268 225 196 256 263 236
235   211 239 277   271 229   273
212   197
217   210 198 275 236 263
235 266 241 207 209 238 188 199 240
279   278 261 236 248   237
274 180 215 172 213 170 271 171 161160 150 151
214 173 189 186 181 252
179 238   260
234 265 276 163 162 153 182 152
228 209 217 200 184 183
260   264 206 215 269 275 194 213
263 278 256 218 273 267 249 273
277   216 231 164 165 201 154 155
270 220 261 266 274 229
227 247 167 166 157 156 252
262 279   237 270 224
238 228 225 190 202 192
234 224 252 244 242 251
227 191 211 208
272 178 257 216 174 255 205 231
267 177 258 220 246
176 204 175 169 168 159 158
193 251 276 253 222
240 203

63

One fucking asshole always has to stand out in a crowd. Find the cunt that's different from the rest. Answer on page 109

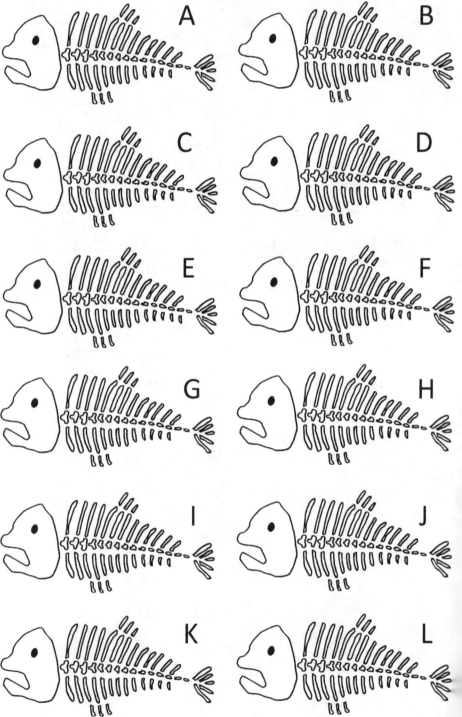

Ever play Sudoku? I bet your sorry ass hasn't!
These are the goddamn rules.   Answer on page 109

Numbers from 1 to 9 are inserted into sets that have 9 x 9 = 81 squares in whole. Every number can be used just once in every, 3x3 block, column and row, so don't reuse that shit.

- Every number can be used just once in the blocks of 3 x 3 = 9 square blocks. Use a number more than once, you fuck everything up.
- Each row of 9 numbers ought to contain all digits 1 through 9 in any order, so don't fucking miss any.
- Every column of 9 numbers should comprise all digits 1 through 9 in any order. Hope you can fucking count.

Here's a hint for your stupid ass: One way to figure out which numbers can go in each space is to use "process of elimination" by checking to see which other numbers are already included within each square – remember, no duplicates, asshole.

		2		9		4		5
		4		8				
3		9	2	4	5			
			1					7
	6	5		2		9	3	
7					9			
			3	5	4	6		8
				7		1		
4		8		1		5		

Bet your ass you can't find the image
hidden in the picture below.
Answer on page 109
Think you can? Color that shit in!
Then see if you're right.

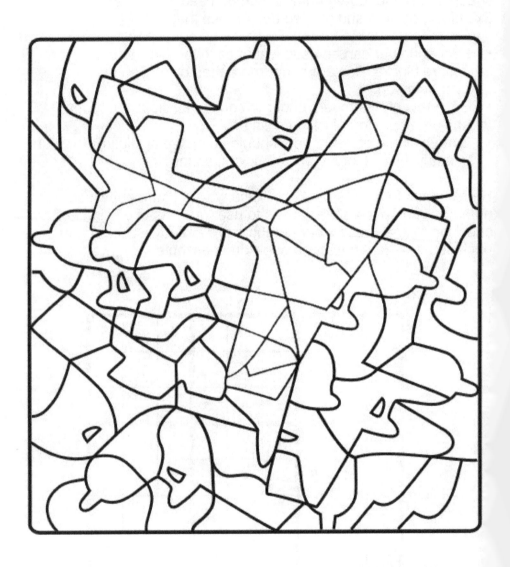

These pictures are not the same, douchebag!
Circle the 14 differences.

Answer on page 109

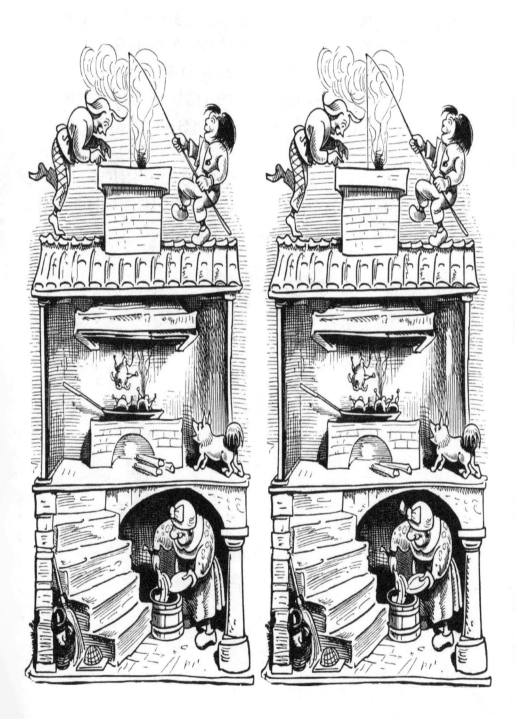

Here are the damn rules of a cryptogram:

You are given a fucked piece of text where each letter is substituted with a irrelevant damn number and you need to fucking decide which letter in the native alphabet is being coded by the numbers you are given.

You need to use logic and knowledge of the letters and words of our goddamn language to crack this shit or your fucked.

Here's a hint for your dumbass. One of the words is: *Much*

Answer on page 109

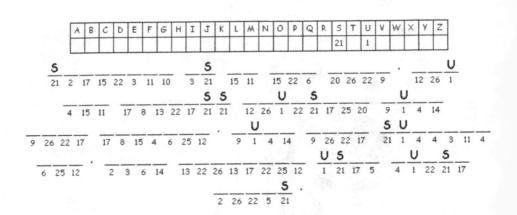

Number Blocks

Answer on page 109

Try to fill in the missing numbers if you can, asshole!

The missing numbers are integers (that means it's a whole number, dumbass) between 0 and 18.
The numbers in each row add up to the totals to the right.
The numbers in each column add up to the totals along the bottom. Numbers can be repeated, so don't get fucked and don't be an ass!
The diagonal lines also add up the totals to the right.
Good fucking luck!

						59
13					14	55
19	2	13		8		45
	10		8	18	20	69
7			2		2	30
0		14	18	10		61
	10		11	2	20	73
60	46	60	52	46	69	51

Find the one fucking image that is different from the rest.

Answer on page 109

70

Answer on page 110

Solve this bitch of a maze. Start in the opening on the top and work your way to the center. Don't fucking cheat your way out.

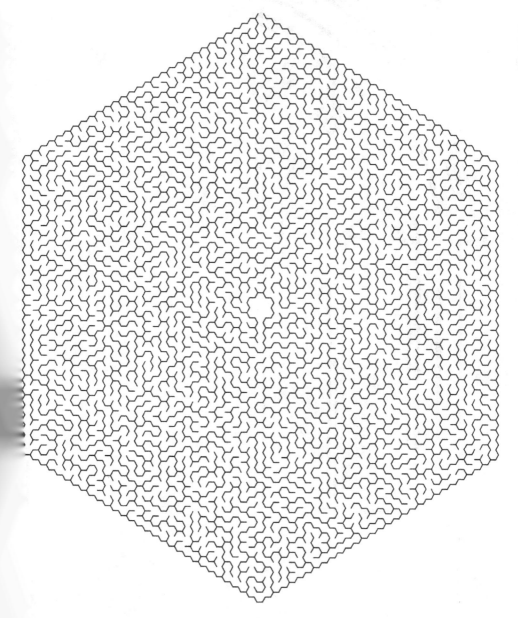

Draw the other half, jackass, and don't fuck it up.

Ever play Sudoku? I bet your ridiculous ass hasn't!
Here are the mother fucking rules.

Answer on page 110

Numbers from 1 to 9 are inserted into sets that have 9 x 9 = 81 squares in whole. Every number can be used just once in every, 3x3 block, column and row, so don't reuse that shit.

- Every number can be used just once in the blocks of 3 x 3 = 9 square blocks. Use a number more than once, you fuck shit up.
- Each row of 9 numbers ought to contain all digits 1 through 9 in any order, so don't leave out any numbers, asshole.
- Every column of 9 numbers should comprise all digits 1 through 9 in any order. Hope you got all that that shit.

Here's a hint jackass: One way to figure out which numbers can go in each space is to use "process of elimination" by checking to see which other numbers are already included within each square – remember, no duplicates, dumbass.

6			8					
		1		6	3			
3		4	5				1	6
	1		3	4			5	
		6		8		3		
	3			5	2		9	
8	9				5	7		1
			9	3		8		
					8			9

Search for the jacked up words

Answer on page 110

Butt   Cretin   Asswipe
Coky   Brainy   Fuckhead
Prick   Cretin   Helldog
Skunk   Fanny   Donkey
Thief   Rufian   Oddball
Wino   Macho   Nobody

```
Q S A N E Y M N Q J M I M M Q W F V F R
O X D J X W Z D G I A P C P C I W K H U
Y J D L J H W G E I G A A C I N D O H F
I B J H L A B J J M H E S V O O I J J I
T N Y A C W M D D S C N Z E K K O R L A
C R H G U Z F B R W W Z Z A K T Y F X N
N H B E W Y S P R A I W M N V Z K H V D
S T T K H E L L D O G X K D N E I D R J
S D H F S H E A A L K Y S H F D A O D T
I A L D F P O H H O J X D H A K Y O E G
E N E K U B U T T R I R H O R I N Y T F
G O A E X Q T M L N R O C A B K L T D C
T X S E O T V F G H V P R V E O E F A T
U U A B O K P I Z E O B D Y J I N J U P
F I S X O F T A W X I C X G P Y L F N V
O U X D Y P U V A W Y E D Q U L B Y B P
F L C L V I R M S M Q O Z Q C L S N R W
S J S K U N K F S M W Y F E X I E I Y N
U R I Y H Z S P W I L S N T G E C A X G
T W N T S E Z X I Z D S B N Q K K R Q N
Y G O O H C A M P O U B X D Z Q O B F J
Y Z C C N P U D E H A O T A Z V C L F N
M A U N G S C R E T I N D T B L Q W A Q
G H G J S V F B K T U F I D U L A E E U
V O W L K B S Z I K J J E Z B C E F P E
U G O G M K Z D P W H M R I S A D N T O
F Q I P X M C W F R G Y N N A F L X R H
N X G J Q D Y S V R E L D H A E F L A W
P J R T O D L U T N R Y H S Q F E I H T
F Z W Y U V D B A D G N D S W U X E O W
```

Tell me how many stars you see in the image, bitch!

Answer on page 110

Draw some goddamn lines from 100 to 173
Don't get fucked by the extra numbers!

Answer on page 110

230
218   278   240   276   260
258   268   233   248   264   121 243
233   233   245   244   120
223   246   242   118 119 122 123
238   246   249   117   124
254   243 245   247   250   237   237
257   253   272   239   125
251   255   274
254   279   255   130 129 128 126
265   236   127
270   226   254   275
271   248   185   249   238
262   264   131   237
238   250   258   259   116 236   265   200
256   241   257   272
242   269   239   212   243
241   214   247   269   266
259   239   115   210   267
244   253   262 114   132 241
239   222   113 195   239   260   269
237   237   226   112 261   271   268   245
236   259   196   256   263   270
236   268   225   111   277   250   245   263
235   110 211   239   197   134 174
212   210   275   263
217 109   198   238 188 175   240
235   266   207 209   177
279   278   261   236 248 176
270   215   213   271   189 199   135   187 178
108   214   217   186   181   179
238   276   273   136   184 183 182   180
234   265   206 148 137   194   213
228   264   159 149
260   169   160   215 138   275   224
263   107   277   278   256   218   273   267 237 249
106   216   231   209   201   193
105   220   261   247 150   266   274 246 252
104 170 168   227   158 151 229   208 139   274 252
262   171   152   140
167 161   238   147 141 202 192
228   276   225 146   251
234   224 252   244   242   191
190   279   166   227   205   211
103   257   216 157   255   231
102 172 267   165 162   258   236   142   220
204   156
101   273 143 229
100 173   251   164 163 155 154   253   145 144   222
240   203

76

One fucking asshole always has to be different. Find that dick.

Answer on page 110

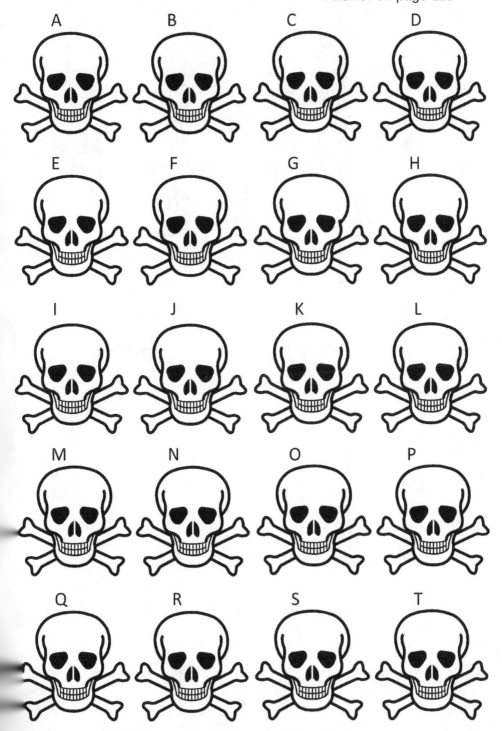

This picture's fucked! Draw each image to its corresponding square to fix this shit or we are all fucked.

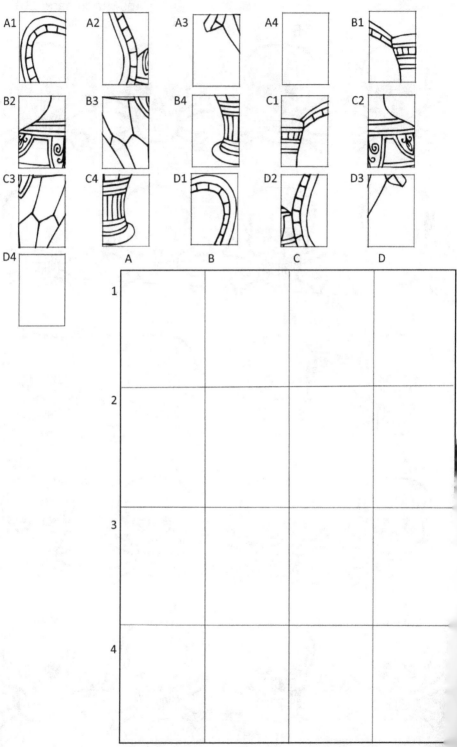

Answer on page 111

Fallen Phrases

Answer on page 111

A fallen phrase is a fucked puzzle where all the letters have fallen to the bottom. They got jacked up on their way down, but remain in the same row. Complete this jacked up shit by filling the letters in the column they fall under. You start by filling in the one-letter columns, because those clearly don't have anywhere else to go in their column, asswipe. Don't make this shit harder than it has to be.

Also try filling in common one-, two- and three-letter words. I even gave your lucky ass an example.

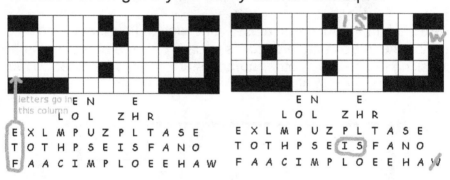

letters go in this column

E	N		E
L	O	L	Z H R

E X L M P U Z P L T A S E
T O T H P S E I S F A N O
F A A C I M P L O E E H A W

E X L M P U Z P L T A S E
T O T H P S E I S F A N O
F A A C I M P L O E E H A W

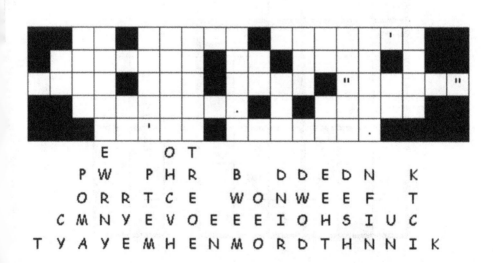

```
        E        O  T
    P  W    P  H  R     B     D  D  E  D  N      K
      O  R  R  T  C  E     W  O  N  W  E  E  F      T
   C  M  N  Y  E  V  O  E  E  E  I  O  H  S  I  U  C
T  Y  A  Y  E  M  H  E  N  M  O  R  D  T  H  N  N  I  K
```

Ever play Sudoku? I bet your sorry ass hasn't! Answer on page 111
These are the goddamn rules.

Numbers from 1 to 9 are inserted into sets that have 9 x 9 = 81 squares in whole. Every number can be used just once in every, 3x3 block, column and row, so don't reuse that shit.

- Every number can be used just once in the blocks of 3 x 3 = 9 square blocks. Use a number more than once, you fuck everything up.
- Each row of 9 numbers ought to contain all digits 1 through 9 in any order, so don't fucking miss any.
- Every column of 9 numbers should comprise all digits 1 through 9 in any order. Hope you can fucking count.

Here's a hint for your stupid ass: One way to figure out which numbers can go in each space is to use "process of elimination" by checking to see which other numbers are already included within each square – remember, no duplicates, asshole.

3		7	1		2			8
				9		7		6
	5					1		
2	8			1			7	
	3						6	
	4			8			5	9
		8					3	
4		3		5				
1			4		7	9		2

The fucked rules of a cryptogram puzzle:

You are given a shit piece of text where each letter is substituted with a irrelevant damn number and you need to fucking decide which letter in the native alphabet is being coded by the numbers you are given.

You need to use logic and knowledge of the letters and words of our goddamn language to crack this shit.

Here's a fucking hint.
One of the words is:
trouble

Answer on page 111

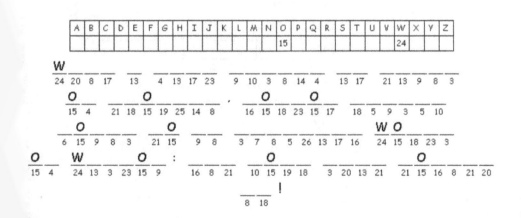

A	B	C	D	E	F	G	H	I	J	K	L	M	N	O	P	Q	R	S	T	U	V	W	X	Y	Z
														15								24			

W
24 20 8 17   13   4 13 17 23   9 10 3 8 14 4   13 17   21 13 9 8 3

O   O   O   O
15 4   21 18 15 19 25 14 8 , 16 15 18 23 15 17   18 5 9 3 5 10

O   O   W O
6 15 9 8 3   21 15   9 8   3 7 8 5 26 13 17 16   24 15 18 23 3

O   W   O   :   O
15 4   24 13 3 23 15 9   16 8 21   10 15 19 18   3 20 13 21   21 15 16 8 21 20

8 18 !

I can't read these fucking words. Unscramble the fuck out of them. Take the letters that appear in numbered boxes to reveal the fucking last word.

IYOFRANPT

SI

HET

NAETELBIIV
3

LIUNICSGTI
1

TUHRCC

FO
2

CINTIETARLUA.
4

| Q | | | | |
| 1 | 2 | 3 | 4 |

Circle the 10 fucking differences. Can you find them all, bitch?

Answer on page 111

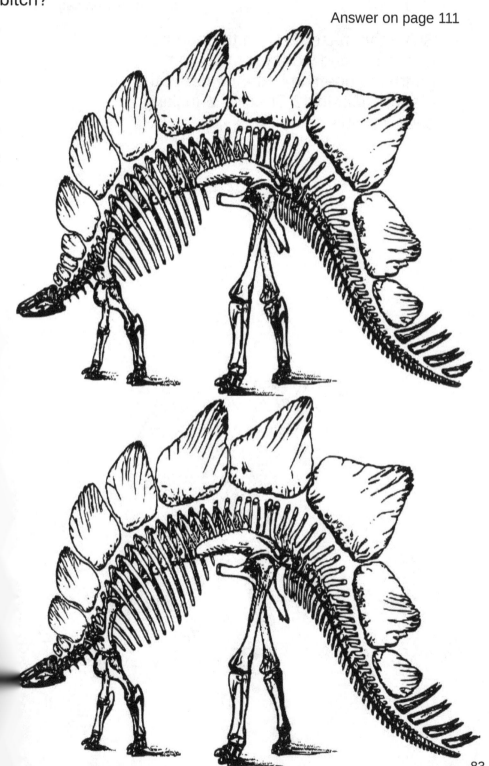

Answer on page 111

Solve the maze. Start in the opening
on the left and work your way to the
goddamn opening in the center of the
triangle. Get lost? Check the fucking
back, dumbass!

The goal of this puzzle is to figure out how the hell you fit the numbered rectangles into the motherfucking large rectangle. And don't even think about splitting those fuckers apart, you goddamn cheater!

Answer on page 112

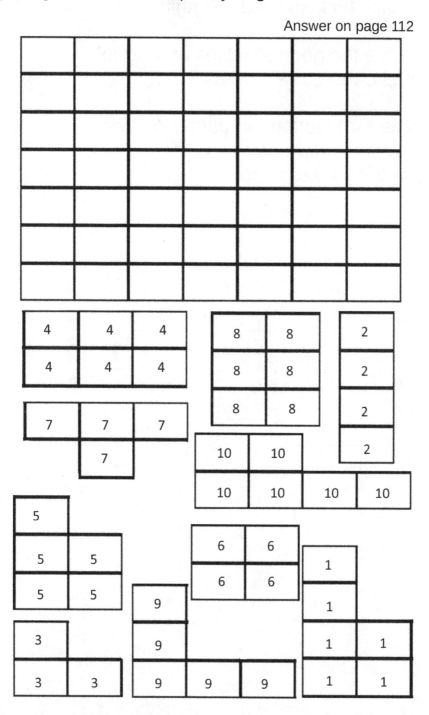

Letter Tiles

Answer on page 112

I can't fucking read this shit!

Move the goddamn tiles around to make the correct phrase.

The three letters on each tile must stay together and in the given order, so don't try to cheat, asswipe!

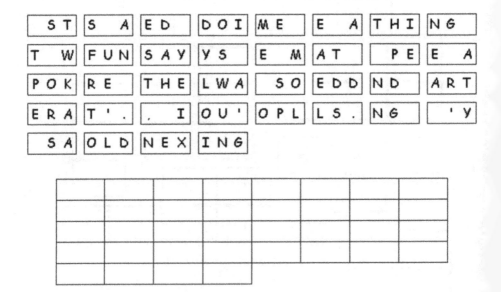

Have fucking fun coloring, bitch!

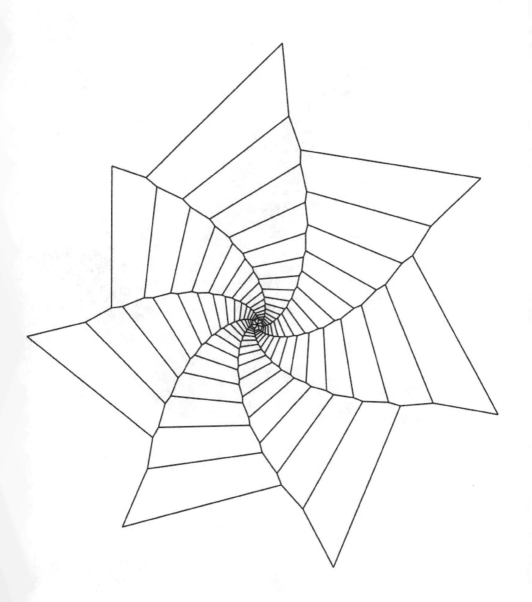

How many goddamn dots can you find?
(This one fucks with the eyes)

Answer on page 112

Find the fucker that's different from the rest.

Answer on page 112

89

This picture's fucked to hell! Draw each image to its corresponding square to fix that shit.

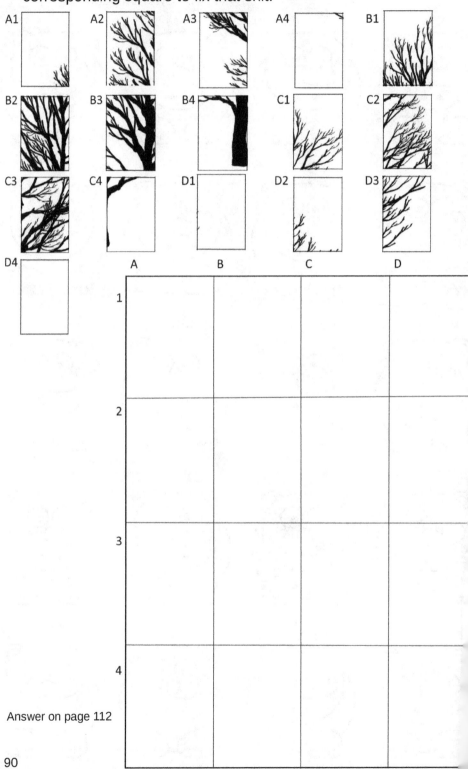

Answer on page 112

Spot the 12 differences between the images, crazy bitches!

Answer on page 112

Connect the fucking numbers from 100 to 127
Answer on page 112

Extra numbers? You bet your sweet ass there are!

161
218 129 230 114 115 128
162 258 268 113 116 240 278 276 243 151
248 264 245 244
223 233 246 242 131
238 246 243 245 249 238
254 247 250 237 150 237 154
257 233 253
251 254 255 274 272 149 239
279 255
265 226 254 275 236
270 159 248 275 166 135
271 185 168 167 249
165 230 236
262 264 132 137
238 160 258 236 265
256 250 259 257 169 272 138
241 212 243
242 269 239 266
241 247 269 267
259 239 214 210
244 171
253 110 111 112 262 118 170 241
239 117 239 136
153 109 222 195 119 120 260
237 237 268
237 261 172 250 245
236 236 259 226 196 256 121 263
268 225 277 271
211 239 174
235 217 156 197 236 263
155 275 240
107 108 212 210 198 236 188 175
235 266 130 173 238 177
106 207 209 236 248 176
279 278 261 133
157 215 213 271 189 199 187 178 179
214 186 181
105 238 146 260 180
234 265 276 273 184 183 182
228 163 200 213
260 104 217 264 206 269 275 194
263 215 122
277 103 278 256 218 273 267 237 139
270 220 261 216 231 209 201 193
227 247 266 274 246 123
262 279 237 270 229 208 124 252
140 238 228 224 249
158 102 225 190 202 192 251
234 224 252 244 242 274 191 142
227 211
272 144 216 147 255 205 231 145
257 101 258 252 220
267 204 229
143 148 152 273 125 222
134 251 100 127 276 253 240 126 203 164
141

Answer on page 113

Search for the goddamn motherfucking words

Ape	Balls	Creep	Bozo
Fake	Idiot	Dufus	Tit
Liar	Minx	Joker	Snot
Nurd	Pig	Satan	Sack

```
U W E I J M                                    S Z Y O Q L
P J O K E R                                    I Z O Q N R
  J F J B A S                                M H R O R M
  G J G W O S                                C J M V J F
    G B V C Z Q                            L G N Y I W
    Q N A P E O                            W W P V V H
      D A O T I Q                        O T E E D H
      T V T F O M                        I V J E W T
        F B A P I R                    T H P K R O
        R L C S W D                    Q F K O C M
          F R K M E I                R L K D W E
          P B C I O I                D B R Q W R
            S A N T B J            N U R D N A
            H S X I Z Z            T I B N I Z
              V P B S L N        D C J J L S
              I I Z S V X        J D U T G Q
                M B U A Y Q    X O S C I N
                Q X X B V Y    E K J Z T R
                  Q K O U J L H W E K A F
                  U P S L L A B I P U F M
                    X O H P P R C I X G
                    W K I D S H U G K J
                      Y R U N O F M S
                      K T F O B I X B
                        G U T D E P
                        X S A G F P
                          E Z W Z
                          P T S S
```

How many fucking hearts can you find?

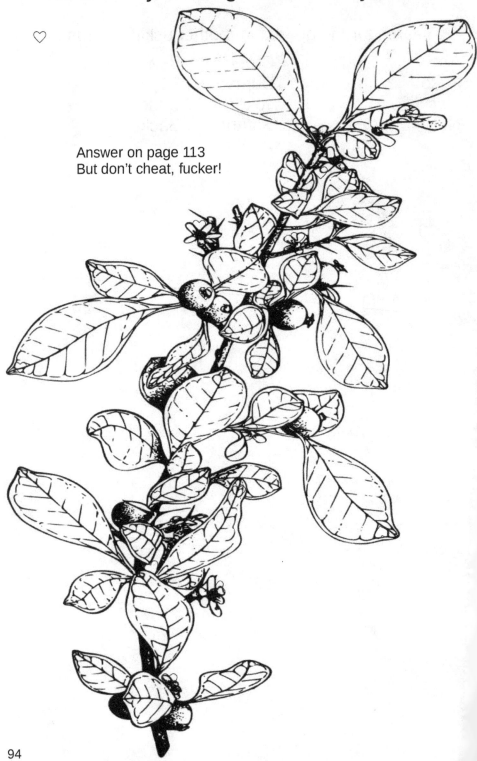

Answer on page 113
But don't cheat, fucker!

Color this shit!

Word Scramble

Answer on page 113

I can't read these wacked words. Unscramble the fuckers. Take the letters that appear in numbered boxes to reveal the best damn word.

LOYH JUSSE NO A KITCS

TOCCISHK CEERHTOURFKM

A RITMEC FUKC-ONT

NFGIKCU HUNCB FO ISTIOD

TAHDISLO

FUKC ME TCIWE NO NAYSUDS

MOHRET-HIST-KUCF

GO SISP PU A EOPR

KUFC YUO

HYOL KFNUNCAFREK

WERHE IN TIACOUKPF

KLFACBULS

Here are the damn rules of a cryptogram:

You are given a fucked piece of text where each letter is substituted with a irrelevant damn number and you need to fucking decide which letter in the native alphabet is being coded by the numbers you are given.

You need to use logic and knowledge of the letters and words of our goddamn language to crack this shit or your fucked.

Answer on page 113

Here's a hint fucker:
One of the words *Insecure*

A	B	C	D	E	F	G	H	I	J	K	L	M	N	O	P	Q	R	S	T	U	V	W	X	Y	Z
4				25															22						

```
 _  '     _   E             ,    _  _  _   A  T      E     T     A
16    26    12 25 6 11 16 12 5    16 26 1   4 22 16 25 24 22   4 24 13

 A  _  _   T  T  _  E    _  _  _  E  _  _  _  E .  _   _  _   A  _  E
 4   6 16 22 22 6  25    16 24 12 25 10 21 20 25    16   26 4 15 25

 _  T  A  _  E    ,  _   A  _   _  T  _   _  _   _  T  _  _
26 16 12 22 4 15 25 12    16   4 26   17 21 22   17 11   10 17 24 22 20 17 6

 A  _  _   A  T  T  _   E   _  A  _   T  _   A  _  _   E  .
 4 24 13    4 22   22 16 26 25 12    5 4 20 13   22 17    5 4 24 13 6 25

 _  T  _   _  _   A  ' T   _  A  _   _  E   _  E
 2 21 22    16 11    8 17 21   10 4 24   22    5 4 24 13 6 25    26 25

 A  T   _  _   _  T ,  T  _  E    _  _  _   E
 4 22    26 8    3 17 20 12 22    22 5 25 24   8 17 21    12 21 20 25

 A  _   _  E  _  _   ' T    _  E  _  E   _  E   _  E  A  T
 4 12    5 25 6 6    13 17 24    22    13 25 12 25 20 9 25    26 25   4 22

        _  _   E  T .
        26 8   2 25 12 22
```

97

Ever play Sudoku? I bet you fucking haven't! These are the wanked rules.

Answer on page 113

Numbers from 1 to 9 are inserted into sets that have 9 x 9 = 81 squares in whole. Every number can be used just once in every, 3x3 block, column and row, so don't reuse the goddamn shit.

- Every number can be used just once in the blocks of 3 x 3 = 9 square blocks. Use a number more than once, your fucked.
- Each row of 9 numbers must fucking contain all digits 1 through 9 in any order, so don't fucking miss that shit.
- Every column of 9 numbers should comprise all digits 1 through 9 in any order. Hope you can fucking count, bitch.

Here's a hint for your stupid ass: One way to figure out which numbers can go in each space is to use "process of elimination" by checking to see which other numbers are already included within each square – remember, no duplicates, asshole.

		1		7	8			6
	9						1	
6				1	3		4	
9		8	7					5
			5		9			
1					4	3		7
	6		1	5				3
	1						8	
7			4	8		2		

Start at the top and work your way the fuck down to the bottom, jackass!

Answer on page 113

Fallen Phrases

Answer on page 113

A fallen phrase is a fucked puzzle where all the letters have fallen to the bottom. They got jacked up on their way down, but remain in the same row. Complete this fucked up shit by filling the letters in the column they fall under. You start by filling in the one-letter columns, because those clearly don't have anywhere else to go in their column, dumbass. Don't make this shit harder than it has to be.

Also try filling in common one-, two- and three-letter words. I even gave your lucky ass an example.

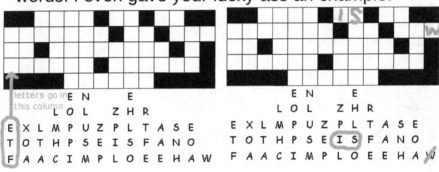

letters go in this column

```
      E  N        E              E  N        E
        L  O  L    Z  H  R         L  O  L    Z  H  R
E  X  L  M  P  U  Z  P  L  T  A  S  E    E  X  L  M  P  U  Z  P  L  T  A  S  E
T  O  T  H  P  S  E  I  S  F  A  N  O    T  O  T  H  P  S  E  I  S  F  A  N  O
F  A  A  C  I  M  P  L  O  E  E  H  A  W  F  A  A  C  I  M  P  L  O  E  E  H  A  W
```

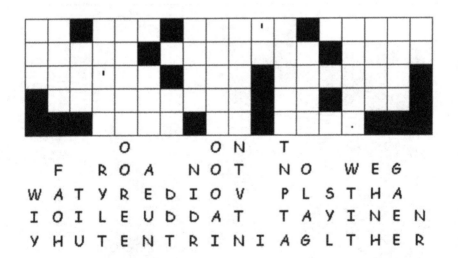

```
        O           O  N     T
     F     R  O  A     N  O  T     N  O     W  E  G
  W  A  T  Y  R  E  D  I  O  V     P  L  S  T  H  A
  I  O  I  L  E  U  D  D  A  T     T  A  Y  I  N  E  N
  Y  H  U  T  E  N  T  R  I  N  I  A  G  L  T  H  E  R
```

Page 1

Page 2

Page 3

Page 4

Page 5

8	2	7	6	4	5	1	9	3
9	1	6	7	3	2	4	5	8
3	4	5	9	1	8	2	7	6
1	8	3	5	2	4	7	6	9
2	5	9	1	7	6	8	3	4
7	6	4	3	8	9	5	2	1
4	3	8	2	6	7	9	1	5
6	9	2	8	5	1	3	4	7
5	7	1	4	9	3	6	8	2

Page 6

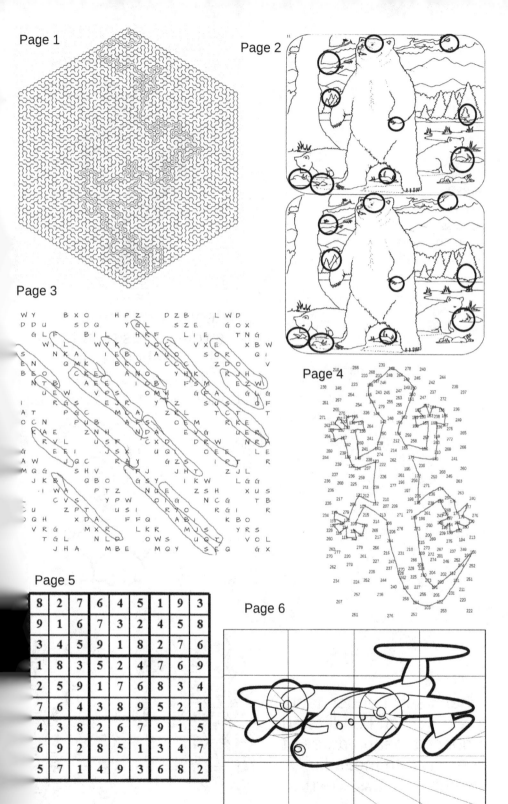

101

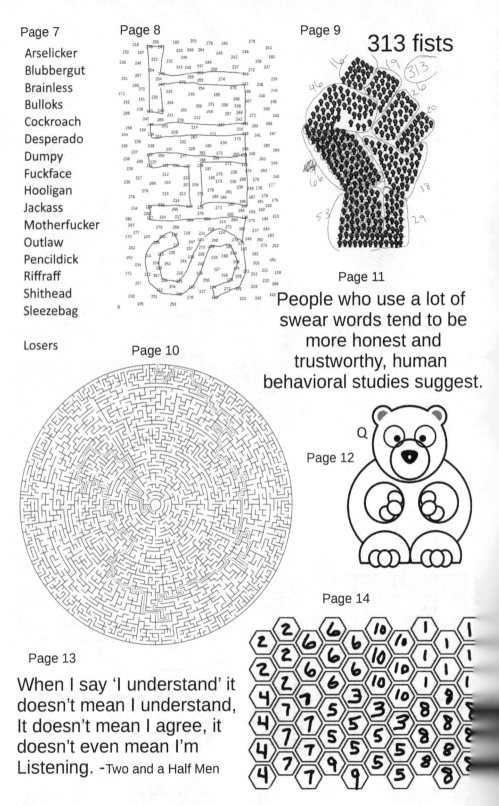

Page 7

Arselicker
Blubbergut
Brainless
Bulloks
Cockroach
Desperado
Dumpy
Fuckface
Hooligan
Jackass
Motherfucker
Outlaw
Pencildick
Riffraff
Shithead
Sleezebag

Losers

Page 8

Page 9

313 fists

Page 10

Page 11

People who use a lot of swear words tend to be more honest and trustworthy, human behavioral studies suggest.

Page 12

Q

Page 13

When I say 'I understand' it doesn't mean I understand, It doesn't mean I agree, it doesn't even mean I'm Listening. -Two and a Half Men

Page 14

Page 15

Assmaster
Bitch
Brainfart
Cannibal
Chicken
Deathlord
Dumbo
Fucknoggin
Lumpy
Neanderthal
Oildick
Ripper
Shiteater
Swindler

Page 17

2	8	7	6	4	5	9	3	1
5	4	9	1	3	8	7	6	2
1	6	3	9	2	7	8	5	4
3	1	2	4	8	9	6	7	5
4	9	5	7	6	2	3	1	8
8	7	6	3	5	1	2	4	9
9	5	4	8	7	6	1	2	3
6	2	8	5	1	3	4	9	7
7	3	1	2	9	4	5	8	6

Page 18

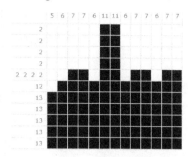

Page 20

162 circles

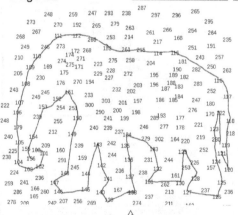

Page 19

				8
5	8	0	1	14
4	4	1	2	11
6	3	6	9	24
3	3	3	8	17
18	18	10	20	23

Page 21

Page 22

Life's disappointments are harder to take when you don't know any swear words

Page 24

25 Dammit

Page 25

Page 26

2	+	8	×	1	10
+	■	/	■	×	
9	+	4	-	7	6
+	■	+	■	-	
6	×	5	+	3	33
17		7		4	

Page 28

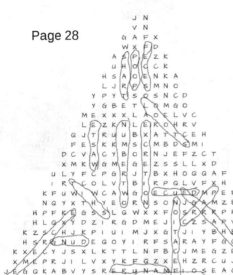

Page 29

Do you ever just wanna grab someone by the shoulders, look them deep in the eyes and whisper "No one gives a shit".

Page 30

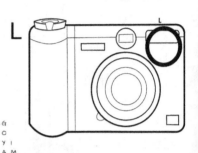

Page 31

You call them "Cuss words"
I choose to call them
"Sentence enhancers".

Page 32

5	9	8	7	2	1	4	3	6
6	7	1	3	4	5	8	2	9
4	2	3	6	8	9	7	5	1
2	3	7	8	9	4	1	6	5
9	8	4	5	1	6	2	7	3
1	6	5	2	7	3	9	8	4
8	4	6	9	3	2	5	1	7
7	5	9	1	6	8	3	4	2
3	1	2	4	5	7	6	9	8

Page 33

Page 34

483 Butterfly

They're= They Fucking Are
Their = Shows Fucking Possession
There = Specifies a Fucking Location
You're = You Fucking Is
Your = Shows Fucking Possession
We're = We Fucking Are
Were = Past Fucking Tense of Are
Where = Specifies a Fucking Location
Loose = Not Fucking Fixed In Place
Lose = Cease To Fucking Keep
Affect = A Fucking Action
Effect = A Fucking Result
Could've = Could Fucking Have
Could of = You're A Fucking Idiot

The Best

Page 40

13

Page 36

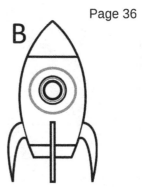

Page 37

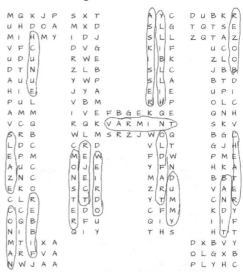

Page 39

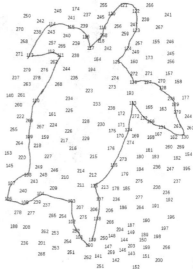

Page 41

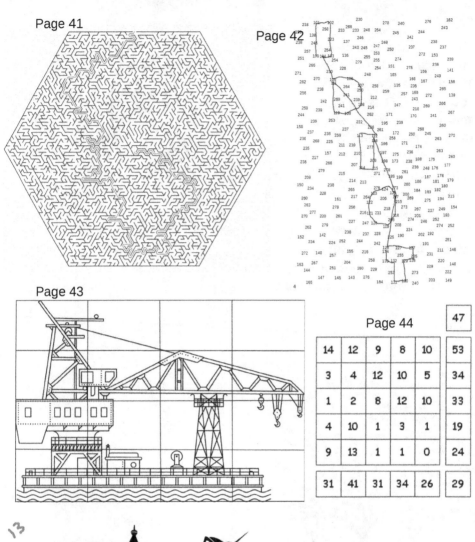

Page 42

Page 43

Page 44

14	12	9	8	10	53
3	4	12	10	5	34
1	2	8	12	10	33
4	10	1	3	1	19
9	13	1	1	0	24
31	41	31	34	26	29

47

13

Page 45

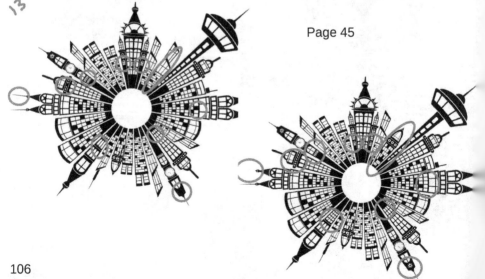

106

I can tell by your sarcastic undertones rude comments and sheer lack of common decency that we should be best friends.

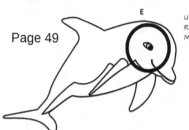

Swearing. Because sometimes "gosh darn" and "poopy head" just don't cover it!

1	-	7	-	2	-	6	-14
-	■	+	■	X	■	X	
15	+	10	+	4	X	12	73
X	■	-	■	■	■	/	
8	-	11	X	9	/	3	-25
+	■	+	■	-	■	-	
16	-	13	-	5	-	14	-16
-103		19		-6		10	

5	8	1	9	7	4	2	3	6
9	2	4	6	5	3	1	7	8
7	3	6	1	2	8	5	4	9
6	7	2	5	3	1	8	9	4
4	5	8	2	9	6	7	1	3
1	9	3	8	4	7	6	2	5
2	6	5	3	1	9	4	8	7
3	1	7	4	8	5	9	6	2
8	4	9	7	6	2	3	5	1

If anybody even tries to whisper the word 'Diet' I'm like.
You can go fuck yourself".

Page 55

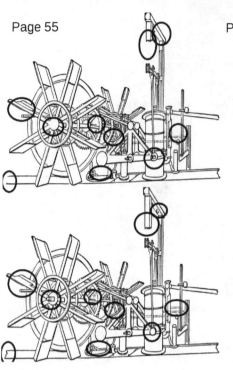

Page 56

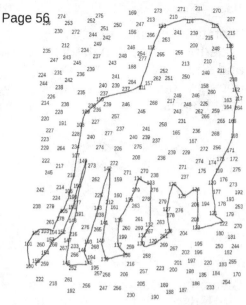

Page 57

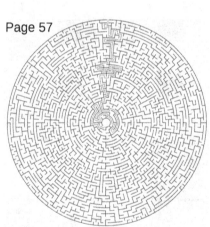

Page 58

There are
213 hearts

Page 61

Page 60

Asshole	Exhibitionist
Bogeyman	Gangster
Brontosaurus	Horsefucker
Chauvinist	Missinglink
Dammit	Painintheass
Dickhead	Rowdy
Criminal	Skuzbag
Drunkard	Slimybastard
	Wallflower

Page 62

	8	1 1	1	0	8	1	8	0	8	1 1	1 1	0	8	2 2	1 1
3 1 1 3 1 1															
1 1 1 1 1 1															
2 1 1 1 1 1															
1 1 1 1 2															
1 1 1 1 2															
1 1 1 1 1 1															
1 1 1 1 1 1															
1 3 3 1 1															

Page 63

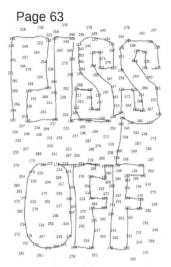

Page 64

E

Page 65

1	7	2	6	9	3	4	8	5
6	5	4	7	8	1	3	2	9
3	8	9	2	4	5	7	1	6
9	4	3	1	6	8	2	5	7
8	6	5	4	2	7	9	3	1
7	2	1	5	3	9	8	6	4
2	1	7	3	5	4	6	9	8
5	9	6	8	7	2	1	4	3
4	3	8	9	1	6	5	7	2

Page 66

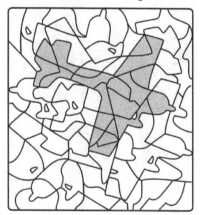

Page 67

Page 68

Swearing is an art form. You can express yourself much more exactly, much more succinctly, with properly used curse words

Page 69

						59
13	7	2	12	7	14	55
19	2	13	1	8	2	45
9	10	4	8	18	20	69
7	9	9	2	1	2	30
0	8	14	18	10	11	61
12	10	18	11	2	20	73
60	46	60	52	46	69	51

Page 70

W

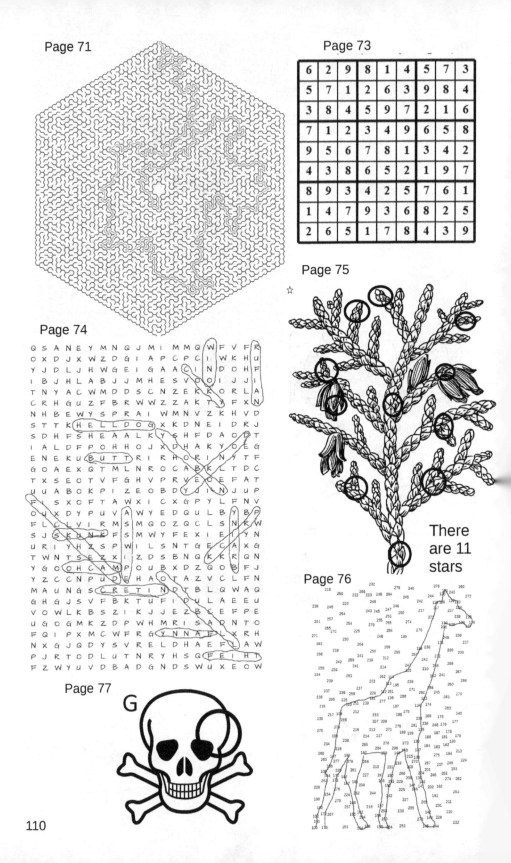

Page 71

Page 73

6	2	9	8	1	4	5	7	3
5	7	1	2	6	3	9	8	4
3	8	4	5	9	7	2	1	6
7	1	2	3	4	9	6	5	8
9	5	6	7	8	1	3	4	2
4	3	8	6	5	2	1	9	7
8	9	3	4	2	5	7	6	1
1	4	7	9	3	6	8	2	5
2	6	5	1	7	8	4	3	9

Page 75

Page 74

There are 11 stars

Page 76

Page 77

G

110

Page 78

Page 79

My phone doesn't correct me when I type the word "fuck" anymore. I think we've bonded.

Page 80

3	9	7	1	6	2	5	4	8
8	1	4	5	9	3	7	2	6
6	5	2	7	4	8	1	9	3
2	8	6	9	1	5	3	7	4
5	3	9	2	7	4	8	6	1
7	4	1	3	8	6	2	5	9
9	7	8	6	2	1	4	3	5
4	2	3	8	5	9	6	1	7
1	6	5	4	3	7	9	8	2

Page 81

When I find myself in times of trouble Gordon Ramsay comes to me speaking words of wisdom.

Page 82

Profanity
is
The
Inevitable
Linguistic
Crutch
of
Inarticulate.

Page 83

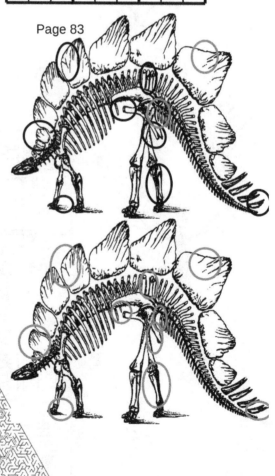

Page 84

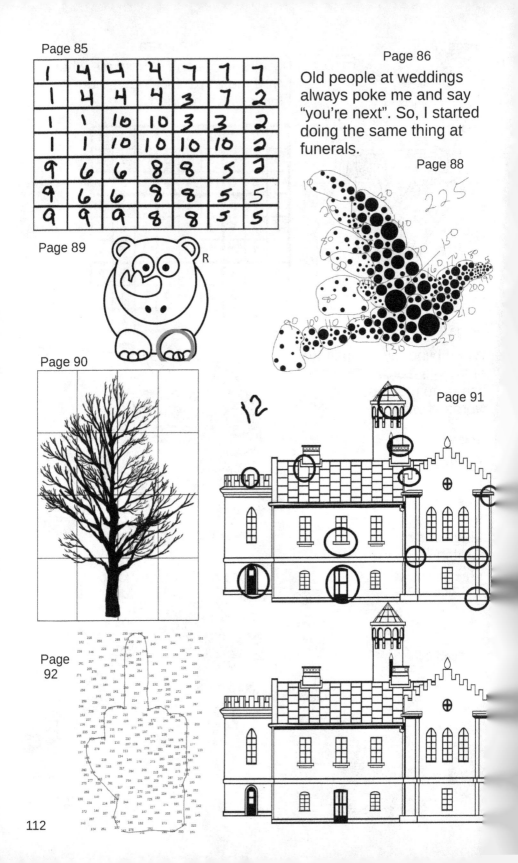

Page 85

1	4	4	4	7	7	7
1	4	4	4	3	7	2
1	1	10	10	3	3	2
1	1	10	10	10	10	2
9	6	6	8	8	5	2
9	6	6	8	8	5	5
9	9	9	8	8	5	5

Page 86

Old people at weddings always poke me and say "you're next". So, I started doing the same thing at funerals.

Page 88

Page 89

Page 90

Page 91

Page 92

112

Page 93

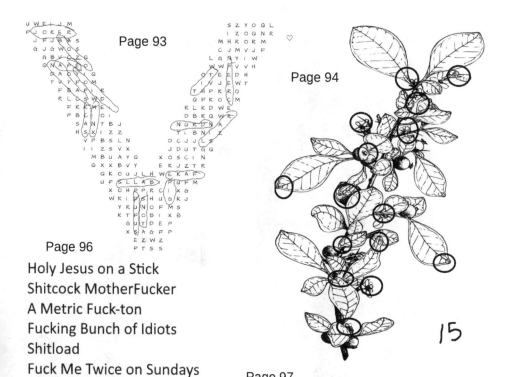

Page 94

15

Page 96

Holy Jesus on a Stick
Shitcock MotherFucker
A Metric Fuck-ton
Fucking Bunch of Idiots
Shitload
Fuck Me Twice on Sundays
Mother-Shit-Fuck
Go Piss Up a Rope
Fuck You
Holy Frankenfuck
Where in Fucktopia
Fuckballs

Fuck

Page 97

I'm selfish, impatient and a little insecure. I make mistakes, I am out of control and at times hard to handle. But if you can't handle me at my worst, then you sure as hell don't deserve me at my best.

Page 98

2	4	1	9	7	8	5	3	6
3	9	7	6	4	5	8	1	2
6	8	5	2	1	3	7	4	9
9	2	8	7	3	1	4	6	5
4	7	3	5	6	9	1	2	8
1	5	6	8	2	4	3	9	7
8	6	4	1	5	2	9	7	3
5	1	2	3	9	7	6	8	4
7	3	9	4	8	6	2	5	1

Page 99

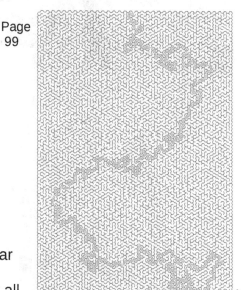

Page 100   If you don't swear while driving then you're not paying attention to the road at all.

Check out these other fun fucking items by the Author:

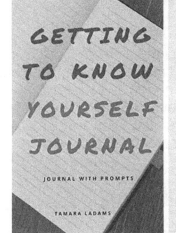

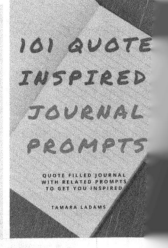

Thanks for your goddman purchase!!

Please leave a review! I would be fucking grateful.

If you **leave a review on Amazon**

And Contact me with your damn info,

I will send you a fucking free paperback book

of your choice from my collection!

Tamaraadamsauthor@gmail.com

Thank you for your support and have a great fucking day!

You can contact me at

http://www.amazon.com/T.L.-Adams/e/B00YSROGC4

Tammy@tamaraladamsauthor.com

https://www.pinterest.com/Tjandlexismom/

https://twitter.com/TamaraLAdams

https://www.facebook.com/TamaraLAdamsAuthor/

https://www.youtube.com/user/tamaraladams

https://www.instagram.com/tamaraladamsauthor/

http://www.tamaraladamsauthor.com

CPSIA information can be obtained
at www.ICGtesting.com
Printed in the USA
LVHW092256091020
668488LV00001B/1